HOW SHALL WE PRAY?

Expanding Our Language about God

LITURGICAL STUDIES, TWO

Ruth A. Meyers, Editor,
for the Standing Liturgical Commission

The Church Hymnal Corporation
New York

Contents

Preface

Liturgical Studies are collections of essays issued from time to time under the direction of the Standing Liturgical Commission. They reflect the fact that our liturgical prayer, while formally set forth in The Book of Common Prayer and other authorized books and collections of texts, is also continually developing and unfolding as it becomes the experience of Christians continuing week by week "in the apostles' teaching and fellowship, in the breaking of bread, and in the prayers."

To encounter the risen Christ in common prayer is often to find ourselves confronted by questions and new perceptions which arise out of the very act of worship itself. It is these questions and new perceptions which are the subject matter of *Liturgical Studies*.

These essays are offered as a stimulus to thought, reflection and further discussion. It is the hope of the Standing Liturgical Commission that they will be seen as a contribution to an ongoing conversation born out of our experience of worship in the Anglican tradition. The essays do not necessarily reflect the views of the Standing Liturgical Commission, and in some cases a particular essay may be at variance with another essay in the same collection.

We welcome your responses to these essays and see them as a way of expanding the conversation as well as helping the Commission to carry out its canonical mandate "to collect and collate material bearing upon further revisions of The Book of Common Prayer."

The Rt. Rev. Frank T. Griswold
Chair, Standing Liturgical Commission

Introduction

Since 1985 the Standing Liturgical Commission, in accord with directives of the General Convention, has been developing inclusive language liturgical texts for the Holy Eucharist and Morning and Evening Prayer. "Inclusive language" was defined to mean "language in which all worshipers find themselves, and their religious experience of God as revealed in Christ, more completely reflected."[1] Much of this endeavor has been focused on language used to speak of God and to God in worship, and it is this aspect of the project which has proved most controversial.

Inclusive language was already a consideration as the 1979 Book of Common Prayer was developed. As the revision process proceeded, there was a growing sense in American society that the generic use of masculine nouns and pronouns was often ambiguous and could be interpreted as referring to males only and not females as well.[2] The Standing Liturgical Commission carefully worded prayer texts and rubrics to use "non-sexist" or "inclusive" language when speaking of human beings. For example, the Rite II texts of the General Thanksgiving at Morning and Evening Prayer include the phrase "for all your goodness and loving-kindness to us and to *all whom you have made*" instead of the 1928 wording "...to us, and to *all men*." In a similar manner, the Collect for Palm Sunday, which in the 1928 BCP began "Almighty and everlasting God, who, of thy tender love toward *mankind*," was revised in Rite II to read "...in your tender love for the *human race*." Rite I texts were not altered, and some generic uses of masculine nouns and pronouns remain in the Psalter and a few other places as well.[3]

viii   Ruth A. Meyers

While concerns about language for humanity were addressed in many places in the 1979 Prayer Book, no attempt was made to eliminate the use of masculine nouns and pronouns for God. However, there were other theological shifts. For example, the new eucharistic prayers give stronger recognition to God's work in creation, and in the Rite II Eucharist, the use of royal imagery is limited to the *Gloria in excelsis*, Nicene Creed, and Lord's Prayer. Neither of these shifts in emphasis is a theological novelty. Rather, the texts of the 1979 Prayer Book reflect efforts to express the fullness of the Christian faith in light of our twentieth-century perspectives on the faith and in response to the particular needs and concerns of our time. In like manner, every previous Anglican Prayer Book has reflected the faith perspectives and needs of the age in which it was written.[4]

In the years after the 1979 Prayer Book was accepted by the General Convention, the use of exclusively masculine nouns and pronouns for God has been increasingly questioned both within and without the Episcopal Church. As masculine terms are more frequently used gender-specifically and not generically, the use of masculine nouns and pronouns for God implies for some a God who is male or has characteristics usually associated with men and not with women.

The issue of God-language is not unique to the Episcopal Church. *The Book of Alternative Services* (1985) of the Anglican Church of Canada expands imagery for God through the use of a wide diversity of canticles for Morning and Evening Prayer. In addition, the final line of the *sursum corda* of the eucharistic prayers in this book reads "It is right to give *our* thanks and praise" rather than "It is right to give *him* thanks and praise."[5] The new (1989) prayer book of the Anglican Church in New Zealand includes a wide range of imagery for God, much of it non-gender-specific, and in a few places uses explicitly feminine language for God.[6]

In the Church of England, the issue of inclusive language in worship was addressed in a seventy-page report, *Making Women*

Visible: The Use of Inclusive Language in the ASB, produced by the Church of England Liturgical Commission and issued in December 1988. The beginning sections of this report address principles for the use of inclusive language, and the remainder of the report (nearly two-thirds of the volume) comprises tables of textual proposals to be used with the texts of *The Alternative Service Book (1980)*.[7]

More expansive imagery for God, although not introduced for the purpose of "inclusive language," is evident in *Patterns for Worship* (1989) and *The Promise of His Glory: Services and Prayers for the Season from All Saints to Candlemas* (1990), two reports of the Church of England Liturgical Commission. Two unofficial publications from the Church of England, *Enriching the Christian Year* and *Celebrating Common Prayer*, also provide a broad range of imagery. The latter book, a version of the Daily Office produced by the Society of St. Francis, includes as an alternative to the *Gloria patri:* "Glory to God, Source of all being, Eternal Word and Holy Spirit: as it was in the beginning, is now, and shall be for ever. Amen." While *Celebrating Common Prayer* is an unofficial text, a Forward by the Archbishop of Canterbury suggests that this office book offers "to the Church a pattern of daily prayer which meets many of the needs expressed by Christians from a wide variety of traditions."[8]

Beyond the Anglican Communion, *An Inclusive-Language Lectionary* was published in the early 1980s under the auspices of the National Council of the Churches of Christ.[9] Many of the major Protestant churches in North America have addressed language concerns as they have worked to revise their worship books and hymnals. The ecumenical English Language Liturgical Consultation, comprising representatives of major English-speaking churches throughout the world, has in its work on liturgical texts addressed issues of inclusive language for humanity and for God. Thus, for example, the Nicene Creed states that Jesus "became *truly human*" (instead of "was made *man*"), and the biblical canticles The Song of Mary and The Song of Zechariah (BCP

1979, pp. 91-3) have been recast to address God as "you" instead of speaking of God as "he," and to speak of "forebears" rather than "fathers."[10] In addition to official worship books, a growing number of publications offer worship materials and music with a wide range of language and imagery for God.

These new texts reflect contemporary theological concerns and the changing nature of the English language. But they also have a strong foundation in scripture and tradition. The work in the Episcopal Church has been an effort not to devise new language and imagery for God but to recover images from scripture and Christian tradition that have not been used in our worship for many centuries.

After the 1985 General Convention authorized work on inclusive language liturgical materials, the initial discussions of the drafting committee formed by the Standing Liturgical Commission (SLC) led to *Liturgical Texts for Evaluation*, used and evaluated in a limited number of parishes, as well as seminaries and two religious communities, for four weeks in autumn 1987. The alternative rites presented in this book were revised in light of the experimental use and evaluation, and presented to the 1988 General Convention. The Convention authorized the texts for experimental use and evaluation throughout the church after a review and some revision in consultation with the House of Bishops Theology Committee.

The discussions of the SLC and the House of Bishops Theology Committee led to *Supplemental Liturgical Texts* (Prayer Book Studies 30), which became available for use late in 1989. Parishes were asked to participate in a process of education prior to worshiping with the texts, to use the texts exclusively for a period of time (at least four to six weeks), and to return an evaluation form and individual written responses for analysis.[11] The responses to Prayer Book Studies 30 provided guidance for further revisions presented to the 1991 General Convention. Most of these texts were authorized for use and published in *Supplemental Liturgical Materials*.[12]

As the work has evolved, its emphasis has shifted. Early attempts to eliminate masculine pronouns and many masculine nouns for God resulted in bland and impersonal liturgical texts, and consequently these efforts were soon abandoned. The focus shifted to "balanced" language and imagery, that is, the use of scripturally based masculine and feminine words, images, and metaphors. But even the term "balanced language" may suggest an approach that is contrived and highly controlled, matching every masculine noun or pronoun with a feminine counterpart. It may be more accurate to speak of "expansive" language and imagery. As we try to speak of the inexhaustible mystery of God, to offer our prayers and praises to this Holy One, we need to find many ways to address God and speak about God.

The development of new liturgical texts has been accompanied by significant theological discussion. The essays in Part I of this collection are offered as a contribution to this continuing conversation about language and worship, in light of the SLC's work in *Supplemental Liturgical Texts* and *Materials*. The authors consider both principles for "inclusive" or "expansive" language and scriptural and theological sources for such language.

In "O for a Thousand Tongues to Sing," Ellen Wondra considers the nature of liturgical language and how that language reflects both the knowability and the incomprehensibility of God. She notes that the materials developed thus far deliberately do not draw from resources found in more contemporary experience and in a diversity of cultures. In proposing that such resources be more fully utilized in the future development of texts, she invites the church to go beyond what have been considered the primary sources for liturgical prayer, that is, scripture and Christian tradition.

The scriptural and historical foundations of the supplemental materials are explored by William Countryman, Richard Norris and Paula Barker. Countryman identifies biblical roots of female images for God, with particular attention to the mother and to the personification of divine Wisdom. Norris comments on different ways in which liturgical language can become inclusive and concludes by offering some historical precedents for the use of such language. Barker examines feminine imagery for God found in Christian tradition and articulates theological principles which guided the use of such imagery and might guide us as we expand our language about God.

Jean Campbell analyzes the use of scripture from a different perspective, that of the eucharistic lectionary. She reviews the extent to which the 1979 BCP Lectionary for Sundays and Holy Days includes stories of women and feminine images for God and concludes by urging further attention to this dimension of the Episcopal Church's liturgy.

Part II of this volume continues the conversation about language and liturgy with papers and dialogue from a theological consultation held by the Standing Liturgical Commission in September 1993. This consultation extended beyond the immediate context of the current *Supplemental Liturgical Materials* and explored theological and methodological issues arising from the development of inclusive language liturgical texts. While all of the participants were open to the use of inclusive or expansive language in worship, they brought a diversity of perspectives. The participants did not share one opinion on any of the individual texts in *Supplemental Liturgical Materials,* nor were they in total agreement as to how the question of expansive language should be addressed in future revisions. The background papers and the excerpts from the panel discussions presented here offer some of the flavor of the consultation.

I extend my appreciation to the authors of these essays for their contributions to this collection and their willingness to respond to the requests of the Standing Liturgical Commission. The SLC acknowledges the work of Karla Woggan, who recorded the dialogue at the September consultation.

Jean Campbell's essay appeared under the title, "The Feminine as Omitted, Optional, or Alternative Story: A Feminist Review of the Episcopal Eucharistic Lectionary," in *Proceedings of the North American Academy of Liturgy*, 1990 edition (Valparaiso, IN: North American Academy of Liturgy, 1990), pp. 59-67 (Copyright © 1990 North American Academy of Liturgy), and is reprinted here with permission.

Ruth A. Meyers
Commemoration of All Faithful Departed, 1993

Notes

1. "Supplemental Liturgical Texts," *The Blue Book: Supplement to the Report of the Standing Liturgical Commission, The General Convention of the Episcopal Church, Detroit, Michigan; July 1988* (New York: Church Hymnal, 1988), p. 95.

2. For example, in 1975 the National Council of Teachers of English issued "Guidelines for Nonsexist Use of Language."

3. Charles P. Price, *Introducing the Proposed Book: A Study of the Significance of the Proposed Book of Common Prayer for the Doctrine, Discipline, and Worship of the Episcopal Church,* Prayer Book Studies 29 (New York: Church Hymnal, 1976), pp. 26-27.

4. Ibid., pp. 36-8.

5. *The Book of Alternative Services of the Anglican Church of Canada* (Toronto, Canada: Anglican Book Centre, 1985).

6. The Church of the Province of New Zealand, *A New Zealand Prayer Book* (London: Collins Liturgical Publications, 1989).

7. *Making Women Visible: The Use of Inclusive Language in the ASB* (Church House Publishing, 1988). I am indebted to Colin Buchanan for his assistance in providing information about this report.

8. *Celebrating Common Prayer* (London: Mowbray, 1992); Michael Perham, with Trevor Lloyd, David Silk, David Stancliffe and Michael Vasey, comps., *Enriching the Christian Year* (London: S.P.C.K., 1993).

9. See, for example, *An Inclusive-Language Lectionary: Readings for Year B* (Atlanta: John Knox; New York: Pilgrim; Philadelphia: Westminster, 1984).

10. The International Consultation on English Texts (ICET), ELLC's predecessor, considered the use of an alternative to "for us men and for our salvation" in the Nicene Creed, but concluded that the alternatives "tended to weaken the main

statement" (*Prayers We Have in Common*, 2nd revised ed. [Philadelphia: Fortress, 1975], pp. 6,8). The Standing Liturgical Commission made use of the ICET text of the Nicene Creed in the 1979 BCP, but opted to drop the word "men" (see Price, *Introducing the Proposed Book*, p. 36).

11. *Supplemental Liturgical Texts*, Prayer Book Studies 30 (New York: Church Hymnal, 1989); a companion volume, *Commentary on Prayer Book Studies 30, containing Supplemental Liturgical Texts* (New York: Church Hymnal, 1989), provided both background and educational materials.

12. New York: Church Hymnal, 1991.

SUPPLEMENTAL LITURGICAL MATERIALS:
THEOLOGICAL, BIBLICAL, AND HISTORICAL PERSPECTIVES

Contributors To Part I

Ellen K. Wondra is Assistant Professor of Theological Studies at Colgate-Rochester Divinity School/Bexley Hall/Crozer Theological Seminary in Rochester, New York.

L. William Countryman is Professor of New Testament at the Church Divinity School of the Pacific in Berkeley, California.

Richard Norris is Professor of Church History at Union Theological Seminary in New York City.

Paula S. Datsko Barker is Assistant Professor of Historical Theology at Seabury-Western Theological Seminary in Evanston, Illinois.

Jean Campbell, O.S.H., is Vice-Chair of the Standing Liturgical Commission and Sister-in-Charge of the Convent of St. Helena in Vails Gate, New York.

"O for a Thousand Tongues to Sing..."

Ellen K. *Wondra*

Corporate worship presumes first and foremost that God is self-disclosing, accessible, and involved in human life and history. Because of this, the language of worship focuses on the presence of God, and it uses images that convey what human persons know of God and how our lives may be brought into greater harmony with God's intentions for us. At the same time, it is *God* that we worship; that is, one who is ultimately incomprehensible to us, beyond both our encompassing and our complete understanding. There is, then, a tension between the knowability of God and the mystery of God; and this tension must be maintained in worship, in reflection, and in holy living, if our faith is to be both authentic and effective.

Corporate worship, theological reflection, and contemplative prayer all have their own appropriate languages, which inform but are not identical with each other. In theological reflection and in contemplative prayer, the tension between the knowability and the mystery of God may be maintained by disciplined attention to the "negative moment" of our naming God, in which we recognize that God is hidden from us as well as revealed, in which we recognize that everything we say of God is partial and limited and therefore not-true as well as true. Such recognition of God's incomprehensibility is imperative. Without it, we readily forget the majesty, power, and sheer graciousness of the living God. Such forgetfulness leads to that overreliance on human capacity and knowledge which is part of idolatry.

Corporate worship, by contrast, focuses on expressing and evoking what we know and experience of God's presence. How, then, can liturgical language help us recognize the incomprehensibility of God? One way is through the multiplication of names, images, and forms through which we address and contemplate God in corporate worship. The *Supplemental Liturgical Texts* and *Materials** (along with the process of development, use, evaluation, and reception of these materials) provide just such a multiplication when they are seen in conjunction with The Book of Common Prayer which they explicitly supplement. The rest of this paper will explain what I mean and why I think it is important that this process continue.

The shape, forms, and language (words, images, gestures) of liturgy matter greatly because our praying shapes our believing and our living. Particularly for members of liturgical traditions such as Anglicanism, corporate worship is the forming ground for Christian belief. It is in corporate worship that we come to know the God with whom we desire closer union. It is there that we encounter the ongoing story of our faith through scriptural and liturgical texts, and it is there that we become part of that story through sacramental participation. It is there that we gain the strength, will, and disposition to live that faith in our daily lives. Our individual prayers and lives are embedded in this corporate worship which spans time and place, joining individuals and congregations together as members of one Body.

And yet we can pray, individually or corporately, only in the images and symbols and gestures—the language—available to us. Much of this language is conveyed through corporate worship and its use of scripture, hymnody, prayer, and so on. But our spiritual formation is accomplished not only in church. The world in which we live is also part of the formative context of our faith, and the

---

Supplemental Liturgical Texts (Prayer Book Studies 30), was published in 1989. *Supplemental Liturgical Materials*, a revision of the earlier texts, was published in 1991. See Introduction, pp. x-xi, for further discussion of the development of *Supplemental Liturgical Texts* and *Materials*.

language of faith derives its meaning not only from our prayer but also from our everyday lives. The Reformation liturgical principle of worship in the vernacular recognizes not only that this is true, but that it has positive value. The basis of that positive value is the fundamental Christian conviction that God meets us in the midst of our history, that is, in the midst of our historical particularities and conditions, and in ways that are accommodated to our contexts and limitations. The Word became flesh and dwelt among us; through that incarnation in human history is our fullest encountering of God.

So it is of great importance that our corporate worship be shaped to recognize the presence of both God and the faithful in particular historical contexts. The revisions leading to the 1979 Book of Common Prayer made great strides in this direction, but more are needed. Some of these are undertaken by the *Supplemental Liturgical Texts* and *Materials*, for example, in recognizing that human sin involves violation of self and of all creation, as well as of other human persons and relationship with God.

The contextual nature of human life is also reflected in the scriptural and liturgical traditions whose continuous use knits together the Body of Christ across both time and space. The fact that these texts and traditions have a historical character may, however, be masked by our conviction that they are important revelations of God who is sovereign over all the elements of time and space. But to say that something is revealed does not mean it cannot be historically shaped, nor does saying that something is historically shaped mean that it may not also be revealed. Indeed, because of the Incarnation—the Word become flesh and living in human history—we can both recognize and embrace the fact that, whatever else our sacred texts may be, they are *also* the work of human persons living in concrete history and responding to the presence of God in that history.

I have already said that God accommodates divine revelation to our conditions and limitations. This is to say that God makes

Herself known in ways that are accessible to our recognizing and available to our understanding. God freely limits what He will make known on the basis of what we are able to glimpse and to grasp. God's accommodation is a manifestation of Her own gracious determination that we be able to delight in the one who made us, to know the one who redeems us, and to love God with the love with which He loves us. Again, it is part and parcel of belief in the Incarnation to affirm that our knowledge of God is historically shaped.

It also must be recognized and embraced that all human works, no matter how divinely inspired and guided, are also both limited and fallible, simply because they are human. What it means to be human is that we are finite creatures living in a created world. We are capable of only partial perception, articulation, and reflection, but we are also capable of growth. In our biblical tradition, for example, this reality is reflected in the two different narratives of the creation of the world, each of which reflects a different understanding of the nature of creation, and both of which differ from other understandings with which we are familiar. This does not mean that we recognize these narratives as any the less true.

In addition to this, there is also sin, that human propensity to turn away from God and each other, to distort our own importance, and to suppress our need of others and our reliance on God. These propensities are reflected in texts and traditions as well, and not just in ways that the Bible itself presents and condemns as negative examples. For example, biblical accounts of divine commands to slaughter conquered non-combatants and scriptural warrants for slavery have, in our context, lost all credibility and are even considered abhorrently contrary to "the Word of God"—even though they are found in something that we recognize as the Word of God overall.

So to say that even the most sacred of texts and traditions is humanly shaped (whatever else they may be) is to say that all such texts and traditions may be affected both by human limitation and by human sin. This does not mean that they are no longer sacred;

rather, it means that they are not inerrant and infallible. And so they must be read critically, with an eye both to the contexts in which they were formed and to the One to whom they testify. The facts that the church is continuously engaged in reform of its life and belief and that some scriptural materials are given relatively little or no weight in our ecclesial life are age-old recognitions of the human shaping of sacred texts and traditions.

There are a number of ways to proceed once one has said that revelation is both accommodated (or relative) *and* uncompromisedly true. One way is to say that a new revelation has come which modifies, corrects, supplements, or even supersedes the old. The problem here, of course, is one of discernment: how do we know which new "truths" are in fact true? Clearly, continuity with already given-and-received truth is necessary. But continuity does not mean identity; it means both similarity and difference. The prophets, for example, reclaimed a faithful God by representing that God in a recast form and in new images. To them, and to those who contributed to the making of the canon, this newly represented God was recognizable as the same God. (To others, let us remember, it was not a god, but a new idol, one to be rejected.) The early church, of course, finally went even further in the same process in its separation from Judaism. Our contemporary processes of discernment and reception are basically the same.

Worship, then, makes use of the various elements of our blessed historicalness to articulate the praise of God and to knit together the Body of Christ. It does so by bringing together multiple materials (word, reading, music, silence, prayer) of different genres (narrative, teaching, exposition, vision, poetry, exhortation, song, gesture) from many times and places (ancient and contemporary, near and far). This bringing together is, and should be, polyphonic. It should have the character of a rich symphony whose harmonies are produced by complex arrangements of individual elements and movements and whose discords serve to increase the abundance of the whole.

Worship should be polyphonic because our human ability to

articulate the fullness of God's graciousness, glory, mystery, and presence is so limited. No single word, image, concept, or story that we have can encompass or convey the full reality of the divine or the wonder of God's coming among us. In part this is so because of our inherent creaturely limitations and the distorting and falsifying effects of sin.

But even more, it is so because of the grandeur and mystery of the divine life itself. Our God is a living, active God who is first and foremost always much more than what we can know or express, and who is *always* creating, *always* revealing, *always* saving, *always* inspiring. Therefore our relationship with God is not reducible to single or immutable theological or liturgical or pastoral or spiritual formulas and narratives. The diversity of our texts and traditions reflects this conviction as much as it does our recognition that our own ability to give voice to the reality of God is bound by the limits of creatureliness and distorted and perverted by sin.

So the language of praise, entreaty, repentance, conversion, and thanksgiving is polyphonic language. It is also figurative. That is, it identifies God with something with which God is not identical—with a rock, for example, or supporting hands; or with wisdom, goodness, or love. It is readily evident to most that God is not identical with any concrete, inanimate object. It is perhaps less immediately clear that God is not identical with more abstract characteristics, like wisdom, goodness, or love. But even when we say that God is the ultimate exemplar of these or other qualities, we are still speaking figuratively. For we know these characteristics most directly and immediately through their human exemplars with all their flaws and failings, flaws and failings that are not, we believe, found in God. Further, while we may say that God is the ultimate exemplar of these qualities, we do not know that ultimacy except in partial forms which are mediated through our historical experience with all its particularities and limitations.

Second, figurative language is both positive and negative. It makes a statement about what something is, but also about what it is not (the latter often silently): to *say* that God is like a raging fire, for example, also *implies* that God is not like that. Sometimes the negation is expressed more directly: God is *in*finite—that is, not finite—or *im*mutable—not changeable.

In figurative language, then, there is a tension between positive and negative, between affirmation and negation. There is also a play, a give and take, an interaction, between similarity and difference, between like and not-like. With this interaction, this play, also comes a temptation to resolve the tension by overemphasizing the positive, stated similarity: to say, for example, that God is love without qualifying the meaning of the term so that it moves beyond what is associated with its human exemplars. In this way, figurative images are taken to be literal statements.

Theologians, spiritual directors, and mystics have long recognized the importance of this tension-laden play of similarity and difference. It conveys to us something of the incomprehensibility of God, the beyond-ness of God who nevertheless freely chooses to be self-disclosing to our perception and understanding with all its limitations and faults.

The play of difference is, in some instances, a play of conjunction, of saying that God is at one and the same time two opposite things; for example, God is the supreme ruler of all and the servant who suffers for the sake of all. This conjunction encourages—even forces—language to expand, to signify more than it might otherwise. The conjunction of the images of ruler and servant recasts the meaning of both, not only in relation to divine activity but also in the context of human society. Such expansion encourages the human imagination, challenging us constantly to envision how things might be true and not true at the same time, how apparent contradictories or opposites might coincide in one harmonious unity. Our reflection is moved beyond the primarily rational to a more contemplative stage where rationality and imagination combine to generate insight and resolution for action.

The play of similarity and difference also guards against idolatry, the exaltation of something less than God into the place that only

God may rightly occupy. For if we recognize that any image or language we use about God is both true and not true at the same time, then no image can become absolute. We may say truthfully that God is our King, but we also must say truthfully that God's way of ruling is most *un*kingly, in that God is neither temporally bound nor reliant on force or coercion for obedience. When we recognize this, we cannot see any king as divine.

In all, then, the fact that our liturgy is polyphonic helps us worship God more fully and truthfully and also turns our attention more accurately to the well-being of all creatures in this created world. The *Supplemental Liturgical Texts* and *Materials* enter into the play of polyphony by deliberately increasing and enriching the type of images used to give praise to God and to foster our companionship with one another. All of this takes place, it should be remembered, within the normative context of The Book of Common Prayer, whose primary imagery is quite different from that of the supplemental materials.

The expansions of imagery in the *Supplemental Liturgical Texts* and *Materials* have been undertaken to recognize specific changes in the context in which our corporate worship is set. The changes most evident to many have to do with gender. But others, at least as important, are also present. The affirmation that Christ's self-offering is made "for all" rather than "for many," the recognition that human social organization is by "tribe and language" as well as by "nation and people," the acknowledgement of the fragility of creation, and the inclusion of reference to the eschatological "heavenly banquet": all these recognize important theological and historical elements that are underplayed even in the 1979 Book of Common Prayer. Indeed, our process of Prayer Book revision should go further in incorporating imagery, forms, and traditions familiar to members of African, Asian, Latin, and indigenous cultures who now constitute the majority of the Anglican Communion worldwide.

So far, however, most of the expansions of imagery have focused on correcting the gender imagery of The Book of Common Prayer and, indeed, the bulk of the Christian liturgical tradition. The expansion of imagery goes beyond attention to language about humans and to pronouns referring to God. However, both of these are of great importance.

The language we use to describe humanity conveys significant messages about the relative importance of men, women, and children, not only in the world but in the church and in the eyes of God. The Rite II texts of the 1979 Book of Common Prayer attend to this concern, by and large, but there is still room for improvement (particularly in regard to children and to creation); the *Supplemental Liturgical Texts* and *Materials* skillfully move in this direction.

The pronouns we use to refer to God either confirm or deny the long-standing theological affirmation that God is beyond "body, parts, and passions," that is, that God is beyond gender, race, age, and the other characteristics that mark human difference and, too often, division. To refer to God only as "He" erodes the credibility of this claim, particularly when our verbal language is seen together with the visual representations that make up such a rich part of our cultural heritage and continue to surround us. The *Supplemental Liturgical Texts* and *Materials* begin to attend to this concern, although (I would argue) they do not go far enough. Use of female-gender pronouns as well as the avoidance of pronouns wherever possible are also needed if we are to convey our conviction that God is beyond gender.

But perhaps of greater importance still is the incorporation of imagery which, though present in our biblical and spiritual traditions, has been omitted from our liturgical usage. The 1979 Book of Common Prayer, like its predecessors, tends to emphasize those attributes of God that are most readily associated with maleness and masculinity in our culture: freedom, sovereignty, reason, and efficacious will, among others. Less evident are attributes like practical wisdom, nurture, loving-kindness, and companionship (particularly in struggle and in suffering), that are most readily associated with femaleness and femininity in our culture. These characteristics, too, are appropriately attributed to God and have been so attributed in both scripture and tradition.

The relative unimportance or virtual absence of some of these attributes from our corporate worship has at least two damaging effects. First, our vision of the reality of God is skewed and obscured, diminishing our ability to recognize and respond to the fullness of what God offers us. If, for example, we overemphasize the reality of God as law-giving sovereign, we may be unable to recognize God's practical wisdom, which made the Sabbath for us rather than us for the Sabbath. We will then be unable to proclaim and embody that same wisdom in God's world. Or, if we overemphasize the fatherliness of God (with the culture-bound notions of authority, jurisdiction, and relative autonomy that accompany it), we may be unable to recognize God's motherliness (with its accompanying notions of intimacy, protectiveness, and presence). It is difficult to say at what point overemphasis becomes idolatry, but it is an ever-present possibility and temptation.

Second, our failure to acknowledge the full range of divine attributes distorts and falsifies our understanding of humanity as created in and restored to the image of God. When we use images for God which are more readily associated with one group of people than another, what is conveyed is that the former group is already more nearly in the image of God than the other. Particularly when our liturgical usage, or more properly misusage, conforms to the unjust systems and ideologies of our cultural context (as it does in its androcentrism), the effect of this is devastating to the humanity of both groups. It gives the favored an exalted view of themselves. It also reinforces the prevalent degraded and degrading view of the other group, affecting social standing, self-regard, and attributed standing in the eyes of God.

The *Supplemental Liturgical Texts* and *Materials* skillfully attempt to restore the fullness of our understanding of God and redress the bias of our understanding of our own humanity. This is done primarily through the incorporation of scriptural and traditional imagery of divine compassion, nurture, long-suffering, and practical wisdom. When these images are used, gender stereotyping is avoided because God is addressed in the second person rather than the third ("you" rather than "she"). Further, all of creation is identified as one ("we," "sons and daughters") and the experiences mentioned as characteristic of humanity are pluralistic (e.g., "we violated your creation, abused one another, and rejected your love"). This practice provides a powerful corrective to the biases of our customary liturgies.

Less evident in the *Supplemental Liturgical Texts* and *Materials* (and deliberately so) are images drawn from more contemporary experience and from cultures that are not represented in the biblical material (Asian, Latin, Native American) or whose contributions to the Bible are not well recognized (African). The enrichment of Christianity by these cultures and by contemporary experience is great. Why, then, should these riches not be added more explicitly to our publicly shared liturgical heritage? It is my hope that, as the development, study, and reception process continues, these important resources will be more fully recognized and used.

It is not just texts that are important here. The process itself is also significant, and it should continue and be expanded both in scope and duration. The play of polyphony found in the conjoint use over time of The Book of Common Prayer along with the *Supplemental Liturgical Texts* and *Materials* contributes to the church's growth in faith and faithful life by stimulating our religious and spiritual imagination and sparking our desire to engage in careful reflection. The conjoining of multiple images, forms, and genres brings to our awareness the incomprehensibility of God, the primacy of God over any idols of our making, and both the limitations and expansiveness of the ways available to us to glorify God and imagine our lives as in harmony with the divine. Some of this conjunction serves to modify and enrich familiar images, adding breadth, depth, and sumptuous harmony.

Some of this conjunction is contradictory and even confusing, as is paradigmatically the case in the parables of Jesus. Yet the twists, disjunctions, and intensifications in liturgical language can serve at one and the same time to disclose the limitations of our language and our understanding *and* to force our imagination out of its accustomed modes. This opening of new horizons can lead us into greater receptivity to new and perhaps different glimpses of God and into greater appropriation of divine grace offered to us and through us to the world that God has made and for whose redemption Christ died and rose again. It is important to the spiritual growth of every Christian to live ever more fully into the reality of God.

It is therefore important that this process of development, use, evaluation, and reception of liturgical texts continue to be done with care, deliberation, and sensitivity. It is also important that ample time and resources be given to this phase of liturgical renewal.

Recovery of underutilized and unfamiliar traditions requires considerable research and study. Moreover, it takes time, patience, and cumulative corporate experience for these traditions to become familiar (rather than occasional novelties). And familiarity is a necessary part of the reception and evaluation process. The gradual incorporation of these elements of tradition may give rise to new imagery, which itself must be tested in light of a number of criteria. These include continuity (though not necessarily identity) with already-received tradition and coherence with generally-held beliefs. Fruitfulness for renewed life for both individuals and communities is also important; this, too, requires time to emerge and be evaluated.

Fortunately, the church recognizes that liturgical reform is an ever-ongoing process, because it is ever needed. The continuing necessity of liturgical renewal arises from a number of areas. Changes in human history, culture, language, and imagery; inherent limitations to human knowledge and the ability to express the reality of the holy; and renewed and expanding relationship to God all affect our worship continuously, both individually and corporately. But our worship is also affected by the certainty we hold that God's grace is beyond our knowledge and our prediction. Therefore, we believe, God's unwavering love toward us will be manifest in ways that will surprise, shock, and unsettle us. But they will also ultimately work our redemption and transformation.

Biblical Origins of Inclusive Language

L. William Countryman

The Christian religion, beginning with the scriptures them-selves, is rich in ways of speaking about God—so much so that no one era ever exhausts the possibilities and there has been room for many shifts in liturgical emphasis and usage over time. Where one age may emphasize "Redeemer," another may stress "Creator" and yet another "Judge." Where people of one time and place may find God most readily intelligible as "Father," those of another may prefer "Light" or "the Almighty."

In our own time, we have seen a strong growth of interest in female imagery for God. This is the development to which the Standing Liturgical Commission was responding in creating the inclusive-language eucharistic prayers offered to the General Convention of 1991 and subsequently published as *Supplemental Liturgical Materials*. Their use of female imagery may sound unfa-miliar to many Episcopalians, since it has had little place in our post-Reformation liturgical usage. Accordingly, it is worthwhile to review the biblical roots of this language.

Names and Descriptions

The names of God in biblical Hebrew (and in the ancient Greek translations) were typically masculine in gender. The one excep-tion was the word we translate "Spirit," which is feminine in Hebrew (*ruah*) and neuter in Greek (*pneuma*). Pronouns referring to God were also masculine. We can best understand the signifi-cance of these facts by looking at them in the context of the culture and history which shaped the ancient Hebrew and Greek languages and to which they gave expression. This short essay is not the place to enter into detail about the socially defined meaning of male and female in the ancient Mediterranean world. Suffice it to say that it was different from ideas that have prevailed in other times and places. It was a world in which male and female deities competed for devotion, a world in which the male head of household served exclusively as the public face of the family and embodied its public life to a degree almost beyond the comprehension of even the most conservative of modern Western people, a world in which women embodied only the inward-looking virtue of shame (somewhat like modesty in our own world, but of far greater social importance), a world constructed on the basis of maximum social differentiation between the sexes.

The language of written texts, of course, may long outlive the worlds that gave those texts birth. As a result, language can come to mean something to readers in subsequent centuries radically different from what it probably meant to its original audience. This is particularly true for those who read the texts in translation. Translation from one language into another already represents an adaptation of a text's original social world (which was fully expressible only in its original language) to the social world implied in the language of the translation. English, for example, has no word that is precisely equivalent to the ancient Hebrew *ab* or Greek *pater*. We translate them "father," and with reason, since the ancient and modern terms do overlap. All three terms designate the "biological male parent." Yet, in a world where the male head of household no longer simply *embodies* the whole family for public purposes, a world where women and adult children have legal and political rights, a world where we are expected to make our own choices regarding occupation, marriage, and even religion, our ordinary word for "biological male parent" cannot possibly convey the power or social significance of the ancient *ab* or *pater*—or his role as public personification of the household and source of identity for wife, children, and servants or slaves. Thus translation is never more than an approximation—even when dealing with something as seemingly fundamental as names of God or the gender of pronouns applied to God.

Names and pronouns, moreover, are not the whole story. Much of the richness we find in the Bible's language about God—and in the liturgical language that is founded on and grows out of it—is embodied not in names but in descriptive language about God. This language is basically allusive and metaphorical in nature. Since our experience of God is, to a great extent, indirect and interior, it does not give rise to simple, straightforward ways of speaking about God. We cannot speak about God in the same definite, specific, easily verifiable way that shepherds can speak about sheep or farmers about wheat or mechanics about internal combustion engines or librarians about books or cooks about recipes and their ingredients. God's transcendence means that we do more pointing toward God, more gesturing, than anything else. We cannot pin God down very securely. Even when we say "God *is*...," we normally follow the verb up with a metaphor: "God is love"; "God is our loving parent."

Even though the biblical writers felt the need, in their own cultural context, to name God primarily in the masculine gender and to refer to God with masculine pronouns, when they entered into the richer and larger field of descriptive language and tried to give a sense of what God is like, they felt free to mingle both male and female imagery. This is the precedent that the present inclusive-language texts follow in speaking about God. In doing so, they explore and make use of imagery based on two principal female social roles: that of the mother and that of the young woman or maiden.

Female Imagery for God in Scripture: The Mother

Ancient Mediterranean culture emphasized the intimacy between mother and young child, beginning with pregnancy and continuing through childbirth, nursing, teaching of the basic skills of walking and speaking, and weaning. While the child was always regarded as in some sense the father's property, the child's close connection with its mother was also emphasized. Indeed, in the polygamous households of the powerful in ancient Israel, a child had a special link not only with its mother but also with other siblings who shared the same mother. The particular character of this intimacy perhaps emerges in the close etymological relationship between the Hebrew word for "womb" (*rehem*) and that for "compassion" or "mercy" (*rahamim*). While usage, not etymology, is always the final determinant of meaning, it would have been very hard for the ancient Israelite to ignore the resonance between these two words.

The Hebrew scriptures often describe God as "compassionate" or "merciful." We also encounter more explicitly maternal language used of God. In Isaiah 49:14-15, God compares himself with a nursing mother:

> But Zion said, "The LORD has forsaken me,
> my Lord has forgotten me."
> Can a woman forget her nursing child,
> or show no compassion for the child of her womb?
> Even these may forget,
> yet I will not forget you.

Or, again, in Hosea 11:1, 3:

> When Israel was a child, I loved him,
> and out of Egypt I called my son.
> ......
> ...It was I who taught Ephraim to walk,
> I took them up in my arms;
> but they did not know that I healed them.

Speaking in their own voices, too, the scriptural authors could describe their experience of God's goodness in terms drawn from maternal care. The Psalmist speaks of himself as depending patiently on God, "like a weaned child with its mother" (Ps. 131:2). Isaiah 66 contains a beautiful evocation of the future prosperity promised to Jerusalem: Zion will bring forth her children without pain or prolonged labor, and they will grow up under her care. Then, in an elegant shift, God actually takes Zion's place:

> For thus says the LORD:
> "I will extend prosperity to her like a river,
>> and the wealth of the nations like an overflowing stream;
> and you shall nurse and be carried on her arm,
>> and dandled on her knees.
> As a mother comforts her child,
>> so I will comfort you;
>> you shall be comforted in Jerusalem." (Isaiah 66:12-13)

The text suggests that God's work is not only like that of human mothers, but actually expressed in the care given by them.

The New Testament, being written in Greek, lacks the opportunity to play on "womb" and "compassion"; yet it retains maternal imagery for God and God's work. Jesus compares his own longing for the salvation of Jerusalem to the protectiveness of a broody hen: "How often have I desired to gather your children together as a hen gathers her brood under her wings, and you were not willing!" (Luke 13:34b; cf. Matt. 23:37b). (Later on, the author of 2 Esdras 1:30 borrowed the phrase and placed it on the lips of "the Lord Almighty.") The Epistle of James combines paternal and maternal imagery in a particularly striking way when it speaks of "the Father of lights" (i.e., of the heavenly bodies) who "in fulfillment of his own purpose. . . gave us birth by the word of truth" (James 1:17-18). The phrasing not only exploits the contrast between male and female parents, but uses the contrast between the distance of the stars and the immediate nearness of the womb to emphasize God's all-embracing power and care.

For the New Testament writers, the use of either paternal or maternal imagery for God is at least partly a way of undercutting allegiance to earthly parents. Jesus admonishes his followers to "call no one your father on earth, for you have one father—the one in heaven" (Matt. 23:9). While the tradition also presents him as reaffirming the commandment to honor father and mother (Mark 7:9-13; Matt. 15:3-9), it more commonly shows him as demanding an allegiance above (and even in opposition to) that given to one's parents. "Truly I tell you, there is no one who has left house or brothers or sisters or mother or father or children or fields, for my sake and for the sake of the good news, who will not receive a hundredfold now in this age—houses, brothers and sisters, mothers and children, and fields with persecutions—and in the age to come eternal life" (Mark 10:29-30). If anything, God's motherhood seems to coexist more easily with that of human mothers than God's fatherhood with its human analogue.

Female Imagery for God in Scripture: The Young Woman

In addition to the image of motherhood, another specifically female social role which was used to describe God is that of the young woman of marriageable age. The historical process by which this happened is somewhat circuitous. To follow it, we must begin by recognizing that most of the biblical documents were written by men and therefore embody, to some degree, specifically male (and, typically, heterosexual) perspectives. For such writers, the young woman could readily serve as a symbol of all that evokes desire—not only sexual desire, but desire of all sorts. This aspect of young women could be evaluated negatively, particularly in the case of foreign women, who might entice Israelite males into the worship of other gods (e.g., the young women of Moab in Numbers 25:1-5). On the other hand, it could and did enter in a positive way into the religious imagery of Israel.

One way to use this imagery positively was to describe Israel itself as a young woman whom God desires. Indeed, in the prophecy of Hosea God continues to desire her even when she herself proves faithless. The Song of Solomon, which probably originated as erotic poetry, came to be interpreted as a lovesong between God and Israel—or, among Christians, between God and the church or God and the individual soul. On the other hand, a different tradition, one that spoke of God as the young woman, grew up in the context of the Wisdom literature. I am referring to the literary personification of Wisdom as a female figure and her identification, in some sense, with the God of Israel. The exact process by which this happened and its precise background in the history of religions are disputed. We have, however, a series of texts which at least display some of the variations it assumed over the course of time.

While we do not know the exact history of the personification of Wisdom as a young woman, it may have owed something to the existence of ancient goddesses of wisdom such as Isis and Athena. It certainly owed something to the fact that the biblical Hebrew word for wisdom (*hokma*) is of feminine gender. It was easy to carry the image over from Hebrew into Greek, since the equivalent Greek term (*sophia*) is also feminine. At its least metaphysical, the personification was simply a vivid image designed to encourage the young male student to pay attention to his studies. Proverbs 7-8 contrasts the figure of Wisdom, alluring and beneficent, with that of the prostitute or adulteress who invites the young man's attention only in order to profit at his expense and bring him to ruin. The student who pays attention to Wisdom will be rewarded with a prosperous, respectable, stable life, in tune with the will of God, for Wisdom has been God's most intimate associate and confidante from the very beginning of creation.

Proverbs stops short of identifying Wisdom with God, though it comes fairly close to doing so. The encomiums on Wisdom in Sirach (or Ecclesiasticus) 1 and 24 do much the same. Sirach appears to identify Wisdom to some degree with Torah. Wisdom "came forth from the mouth of the Most High, and covered the earth like a mist," but then took up her particular residence with Israel (Sir. 24:3, 8). Another strand of Jewish thinking, however, went further and spoke of Wisdom as somehow both distinguishable and indistinguishable from God. Wisdom of Solomon describes her as "a reflection (*apaugasma*) of eternal light." The passage continues:

> Although she is but one, she can do all things, and while remaining in herself, she renews all things; in every generation she passes into holy souls and makes them friends of God, and prophets;
>
> ....
>
> She reaches mightily from one end of the earth to the other, and she orders all things well. (Wis. 7:26-27; 8:1)

Wisdom also presided over the exodus and the formation of the people of Israel (e.g., Wis. 10:15-21). This description seems to make of Wisdom a kind of personified attribute of God, in some ways borrowing functions of the Spirit. She is functionally the same as God and yet can be thought of or spoken of as different from God.

This highly developed image of Wisdom as, in some sense, identifiable with God was one of the resources available to early Christians as they attempted to explain who and what Jesus was and why he was so important. Already in the way Jesus' own teaching was preserved we find evidence that he was being understood as incarnate Wisdom. In Luke 7:31-35, we find a saying in which Jesus was explaining the difference between his ministry and that of John the Baptist; he concludes by saying, "Wisdom is vindicated by all her children," apparently meaning that both he and John the Baptist were to be seen as children of Wisdom. In the parallel version of the saying in Matthew 11:16-19, however, the language is a bit different: "Wisdom is vindicated by her *deeds*." Behind this shift lay a conviction that the works of Jesus were *per se* the works of Wisdom. A similar line of thinking may lie behind Paul's reference to Jesus as "the wisdom of God" (1 Cor. 1:24).

There can be little doubt that the incarnational christology of John and some other New Testament writers owes a debt to the kind of Wisdom theology exemplified in Wisdom of Solomon. The Gospel of John is clearest on the matter. It begins by celebrating the *Logos* (conventionally translated "Word") of God, who "was with God and was God" (John 1:1). Like Wisdom, the Logos is both identical with God and distinguishable from God. Also like Wisdom, the Logos is the agent of God's creative work (John 1:3). Indeed, one may best understand the Logos as simply being Wisdom under another name—a shift for which we cannot name a simple reason. It can already be found in Wisdom 18:14-16, where God's emissary, functionally the same as Sophia (Wisdom), but here an agent of destruction, is named Logos.

The same pre-existent divine persona appears in Hebrews 1:1-4 and Colossians 1:13-17 under the name of "Son." In these passages, too, this persona is the agent of creation and is described as having the greatest possible likeness to God, being "the image (*eikon*) of the invisible God" (Col. 1:15) or "the reflection (*apaugasma*) of God's glory and the exact imprint of God's very being" (Heb. 1:3, probably alluding to Wis. 7:26). The same thinking may well lie behind Paul's description of Jesus in Philippians 2:6: "who, though he was in the form (*morphe*) of God, did not regard equality with God as something to be exploited."

In short, the divine hypostasis (to use later theological language) who became incarnate in Jesus is none other than Wisdom, even though the New Testament writers more commonly apply to her the names "Logos" (Word) and "Son." The aspect of God personified by Jewish writers as an attractive young woman provided the groundwork for later Christian understanding of the Trinity. The fact that masculine names (Logos and Son) superseded the feminine one may mask the continuity, but the attributes of both are the same. The earlier Wisdom christology evident in the saying which Luke and Matthew report about Wisdom's "children" or "works" achieved a more refined form in a doctrine of Incarnation, which understood Wisdom/Logos/Son as having actually become one with humanity in Jesus. Even with the substitution of masculine terms, the basic source of this incarnational theology was rooted in the earlier imagery of God as a desirable young woman.

Female Imagery for God in the Inclusive-Language Eucharistic Prayers

With the preceding discussion of biblical imagery in mind, we can now look at a few specific elements in the inclusive-language eucharistic texts to see how the biblical background has informed them. Each eucharistic prayer utilizes the biblical resources in a distinctive way.

Eucharistic Prayer 1 draws primarily on imagery describing God as mother. The line "source of life and fountain of mercy" can be read as alluding to the Hebrew word-play of *rehem* (womb) and *rahamim* (mercy), mentioned above. The preface provided for general use alludes to the mother's role in feeding the child. It can also be understood as returning thereafter to the imagery of the womb. The phrase "knit us into one body" is most obviously an allusion to Ephesians 4:16 and Colossians 2:2, 19, where "body" is used in this corporate sense. The reader of English translations, however, will also recall the familiar phrase of Psalm 139:13, where the Psalmist says to God,

> "For it was you who formed my inward parts;
> you knit me together in my mother's
> womb.

The knitting together of the church as Christ's Body is thus likened to the formation of the individual person in the womb. The repeated reference to humanity as formed in God's image may remind us that this divine image is found equally, according to Genesis 1:26-27, in both women and men. This leads on naturally to the prayer's reference to Abraham and Sarah, reminding the hearer that God has fulfilled God's promises through the agency of both women and men.[1]

Eucharistic Prayer 2 also emphasizes maternal imagery for God, speaking (in language derived from Hosea and Isaiah) about God's lasting care for the children God has borne. Just as the scriptures could speak of God's motherhood as finding expression in human motherhood, so, too, this prayer particularly raises up the motherhood of Mary and its role in the history of salvation.[2]

Eucharistic Prayer 3 incorporates Wisdom imagery, specifically making the identification between Wisdom and Word (Logos) not once but twice: "She [Wisdom] is your Word from the beginning" and, again, "Holy is your eternal Word, whom you first revealed as your Wisdom." This emphatic and, as explained above, scripturally grounded identification of Wisdom with Word prepares the way for the announcement of the Word's incarnation, through Mary, in Jesus. The language describing this incarnation as a divine self-humbling or self-emptying, leading to death on the cross, comes from Philippians 2:5-8. Wisdom is described in the invariable preface in terms drawn from a variety of sources, of which I offer only a selection here: she is agent of creation (Prov. 8:22-31; Wis. 8:1, 9:9; John 1:3), "reflection" (*apaugasma*) of God's glory (Wis. 7:26; cf. Heb. 1:3), "image" of God's goodness (Wis. 7:26; cf. Col. 1:15; Heb. 1:3), leader of the Exodus (Wis. 10:15-21), and the power who creates holy souls and prophets (Wis. 7:27).[3]

Conclusion

The three eucharistic prayers under discussion here break new ground in the way Episcopalians speak to and of God. They do so, however, by returning to and reclaiming riches of descriptive language found in the scriptures themselves. If they seem to make a new departure, that is only because they are restoring something long lost out of liturgical use. The imagery of God as mother and the attractive figure of God's Wisdom are not truly new to us, for they are familiar from our reading of the Bible. To recover them liturgically is simply to reconnect with some neglected roots.

Notes

1. "Eucharistic Prayer 1," in *Supplemental Liturgical Materials* (New York: Church Hymnal, 1991), pp. 35-8.

2. "Eucharistic Prayer 2," in *Supplemental Liturgical Materials*, pp. 39-42.

3. "Eucharistic Prayer 3" was presented to the 1991 General Convention (see "Report of the Standing Liturgical Commission," in *The Blue Book: Reports of the Committees, Commissions, Boards and Agencies of The General Convention of the Episcopal Church*, 1991, pp. 268-70) and referred back to the Standing Liturgical Commission for evaluation, study, and refinement in consultation with the House of Bishops Committee on Theology, but was not authorized for experimental use.

Inclusive Language Liturgies
General Theological Seminary
Alumni Day, 1990[1]

Richard Norris

1

I have been asked to speak this afternoon about the business of "inclusive language" in liturgy—a subject that is much in the air these days, not least because of a set of liturgies that have been authorized, at the behest of the Standing Liturgical Commission, for experimental use in the Episcopal Church. I need hardly add—but I will nevertheless—that these liturgies, like the project they represent, are, and will no doubt continue to be, controversial. There will be people—perhaps in this very place—who would, if left to their own devices, prefer simply to ignore these creations and, with them, the issue they try to resolve. There will be others, less repressed, who will be openly and vocally hostile to them—who will find in them, and in their every turn of phrase, not an idle and captious annoyance, but a genuine offense, a thorough-going repudiation of the dogmatic and liturgical tradition by which the church has habitually lived. But then there are others, equally numerous, who will be critical of these liturgies for just the opposite reason: that they represent little more than a tentative first step in the direction of a truly inclusive liturgical idiom—a step to be welcomed, no doubt, but not to be too loudly or indiscreetly applauded, lest the impression be given that they will in the end prove satisfactory. And finally, there will no doubt be a few, a very few, who actually like these liturgies and think they have accomplished what is necessary.

In the face of all this difference of opinion and the commitments, not to say passions, that shape it, I wonder sometimes what kind of fool one has to be to stand up in public and address the problems that these liturgies raise. I have no real answer to that question, but there are two things that embolden me thus to play the fool. The first, which I submit simply by title, is the fact that I am a tenured professor and am therefore less liable to the consequences of my foolishness than some others might be. The second—more interesting if not more important—is that among the various points of view just sketched, there is none with which I find myself in complete sympathy. I do not think that the issues of inclusive language in the liturgy are trivial or unimportant, or that they will go away. I do not think that the use of inclusive language in the liturgy in and of itself contravenes, contradicts, or overthrows the doctrinal tradition that the liturgy embodies. On the other hand, while I have a superabundance of nits to pick at in the texts before us, I do not think that the enterprise they represent is a mere first step toward a genuinely and ideally "pure" liturgical language. I think that what they are making a stab at is exactly the right thing—even though I do not find them, in their present shape, satisfactory. And because this position, or set of positions, strikes me, on reflection, as curious if not perverse, I am emboldened to explain it as best I can. And so to work.

2

Now I do not think that anyone here will doubt the seriousness of the questions we are taking up. The documents before us are liturgies, some version of which will probably be licensed by the General Convention to serve as possible alternatives to the equivalent liturgies in the 1979 Book of Common Prayer. Since the Episcopal Church, unlike some other Christian bodies, publicly defines and confesses its faith *only through the forms of worship—the liturgies—which it enjoins upon congregations or licenses for their use*, it has to be said quite clearly from the start that neither the Standing Liturgical Commission in proposing, nor we ourselves in weighing and testing, these forms of worship are playing some cheerful, inconsequential, or peripheral game. We are, to phrase the matter briskly, getting at the church where it lives. The church's liturgies are public enactments in word and deed of the new life with God that is conferred on us in Christ through the power of the Spirit. Therefore we cannot ask of these—or for that matter any other—liturgies merely whether they are nice, or whether they suit or do not suit our current feelings about things, or whether they are just what "our people" have been waiting for (whatever those "other people" may think). The question is whether these liturgies as enacted articulate and manifest that same new life with God in Christ which has been attested down the centuries in all the great liturgical traditions of the church, and therefore whether they are, in principle, liturgies *for everyone* and not just for "us," whoever "we" happen to be.

Furthermore, the matter of so-called "inclusive language" is connected with this question, not indirectly but directly. We may like or dislike, criticize or approve, this or that turn of phrase, this or that specific formulation of an idea; but the *ultimate* issue is one of principle. Does the use of inclusive language obscure the meaning of the Gospel that Christian liturgy enacts, or does it clarify something about the Gospel that other ways of talking and praying and praising run the risk of hiding? This question ought, I think, to take a certain precedence in our minds over the equally real but nevertheless secondary matter of how well these liturgies are crafted.

3

With this issue in mind, we can go on to ask the basic question: what is intended by the phrase "inclusive-language liturgies"? Now

I realize that for ordinary, practical purposes we all know what that expression means. It refers to liturgies that reflect, in the language, the symbols, and even the names they use, the fact that the story they tell, the faith they express, and the relation to God they enact are now and always have been as much the business of women as of men. That much is clear. But behind that handy definition there lurks the more difficult question: *when is language "inclusive" and what makes it so?*

The easy way to come at this question is to start with the situation that the use of "inclusive language" tries to remedy. The fact of the matter is that the English language, not to mention most of the others in which Christian liturgy has been done, has tended automatically to feature the male half of the human race. Furthermore, this linguistic fact, as we know, reflected a social fact: that women, however significant and even prominent they may have been in the actual business and life of a society, were systematically denied under normal circumstances any *public* place or role. Women, you might say, were always background, presupposed but scarcely ever noticed. It was always men for whom a stage was available to strut and fret upon; women stayed in the wings.

But this is no longer true, is it? For various reasons that I would not even attempt to analyze, this social situation has been changing slowly; and in our time and place, women are finally getting their rights. The stage is open to them, and they too may strut and fret upon it along with their fathers, brothers, husbands, and sons. At last, you might say, the whole human race is out in the open, visible in the workplace, in politics—and in the public doings of the church. Visible, that is, almost everywhere except in our language, which still reflects the circumstances and attitudes of the past. Insofar as our language is itself a public stage, women still do not figure there very easily or obviously. The human race is still, for the most part, called "*man*kind"; a human person not explicitly known to be female is always "he"; the assembled church still tends to be "brethren." Now, though, that we have more than one Right

Reverend *Mother* in God (a comforting thought), perhaps it is time to let women—the feminine, if you like—*show* in the language of our liturgies.

And here we are back to our original question—the question of what is involved in such a project, and to this question I now turn.

4

The project that goes under the name of "inclusive language" really involves—or so it seems to me—several distinct tactics. I will identify them here and then briskly enlarge upon them. First, it involves cultivation of the art of being appropriately noncommittal. Second, it involves the positive practice of inclusion. Third, it involves a systematic attempt at disarming certain kinds of expressions by interpretation. No doubt this sounds abstract and formidable, but let me explain.

First of all, then, *the art of being appropriately noncommittal:* what this tactic entails can be stated quite simply. When one is referring to a group of human persons that, whether in fact or in principle, includes both women and men; or when one is referring to an undefined individual that might turn out to be either a man or a woman: in these circumstances one employs *noncommittal* language. Thus when the scriptures say "Thou shalt not steal," the word "thou" is presumably meant to address women as well as men and is, in the sense required, noncommittal. Similarly, when Jesus says "Blessed are those who hunger and thirst for righteousness," the word "those" is noncommittal, and no suggestion is made that there is some class of persons—women, perhaps—who cannot achieve this particular form of beatitude. But when Jesus says, in the English of the Revised Standard Version, "He who has ears to hear, let him hear," the word "he" is *not* noncommittal and might be taken to suggest that the message is only for males. Presumably, though, Jesus meant: "Let anyone who has ears to hear pay attention!" And *that* is, in English, noncommittal.

The art of being noncommittal, however, is only part of the game—and, I suspect, a merely preliminary and ground-clearing move. Sometimes, indeed, it is hard to practice. There come moments when we find ourselves compelled to employ rather clumsy turns of expression like "he or she," which are interesting because they occupy a borderline between the noncommittal and the properly *inclusive*. This is our second—and, I think, more important—tactic: the practice of *positive inclusion*. This tactic encompasses a number of different possible moves. For example, it is important to *name* women in the liturgy—women who have had a role in the history of salvation. Why can we not have Sarah as well as Abraham? Paul remembers "our sister Phoebe," not to mention Prisca, whom he calls his fellow-worker in Christ. Why should not we remember them? Why do our memories expunge the women who count among the apostolic persons, the founders of the churches? But more even than this: why do we not imitate the scriptures—and, as I shall try to show in a moment—the teachers of the early church, in using imagery drawn from women's roles and activities and experiences to express our relationship to God, or God's to us? If the prophet Hosea can picture God as suffering birth-pangs, why cannot we? If Jesus can picture himself as a mother hen gathering her chicks, why cannot we picture him that way? Perhaps we are hiding something from ourselves. One of the most interesting things about these liturgies we are undertaking to study is their attempt to do just this sort of thing, and it might be useful to read through them with view to picking out the phrases and expressions that figure our relation to God in what one might call feminine terms.

But there is a third tactic: the tactic of what I have called *disarming*, and this needs more careful explanation. Many contemporary experiments in inclusive language are based almost exclusively on an extension of what I have called the tactic of being noncommittal. That is, they have tried in various ways to "neuter" not merely our use of words that refer to men and women indifferently but also, and in particular, the language in which we speak of or address God. In line with this policy, they have devised regular noncommittal substitutes for words like "Father" as applied to God, or "Son" as applied to Jesus—"Creator," for example, and "Child." Now it may be that such a procedure is in many cases and in many circumstances justified, and I do not want to argue here that it is not. What I do want to suggest is that as a *blanket policy*, this cultivation of the noncommittal will not do, and for very good reasons. The most obvious reason is that God is not a creature. "My ways are not your ways," someone once said, and this is a good point to keep firmly in mind. It may well be, then, that the convenient division of the cosmos into things masculine, feminine, and neuter does not work with God in the same way it works with us and our fellow creatures. Yet and nevertheless it is the case—and here is a second reason—that gender-related symbols, images, and metaphors are essential carriers and interpreters of our relationship to God. What is more, as I shall argue in a moment, Christian tradition, even in its most old-fashioned forms, depends not only on masculine but also on feminine imagery for its apprehension of God. So where this issue is concerned we have some thinking to do.

The trouble, I suspect, lies in our failure to understand *first* that when we speak of God we invariably do so in language that is symbolic and metaphorical; and *second* how it is that our symbols and metaphors work, how it is that we normally, and quite thoughtlessly, *use* them, whether we are speaking theologically or not. Take a cheerfully nonliturgical, nontheological example. We speak, not infrequently, of an electrical *current* which *runs* through a wire, and we do so carelessly and without thought. Similarly, we see nothing odd in saying to someone: "Be careful! The *power* is on and that wire is *alive*."

Now when we talk in these singular ways, we are not just decorating our speech with artful figures to achieve some effect. On the contrary, the metaphors we use are meant with dead seriousness: they are our way of grasping and conveying a real state of affairs.

In other words, we are speaking in the only way we *can* speak about these matters, and we intend our words to say something that is true. If you suppose otherwise, ask yourself whether you would touch a wire that some reliable person had reported to be "alive." Nevertheless on reflection we would admit that the statement is some kind of figure of speech: the wire, we might say, is not *literally* alive, any more than electricity *literally* runs. Suppose that a child, though, hearing us talk in this manner, concluded that since it runs, electricity must have feet. What would we reply? Well of course we would correct the child. We might, for example, say something like this: "When I say that electricity *runs* through a wire, I mean that it *flows*." Thus, interestingly, we use a metaphor to explain, interpret, and control another metaphor: we do not give up our original figure—we use another figure to disarm it, to deprive it of unintended or inappropriate implications.

Here then is what I mean by "disarming": interpreting, and hence limiting the meaning of, one metaphor with another. And since our talk about God, like our talk about electricity, is almost entirely a matter of metaphor (for we cannot *define* infinite Goodness in literal terms), this tactic is used constantly in theology even though we seldom notice it. There is, for example, a hymn in Paul's Letter to the Philippians (2:5-11) whose whole meaning turns on the tactic of disarming. In that hymn, Jesus is presented in two roles: that of Lord and that of Servant or Slave. Now in Paul's experience, and that of his readers, these two roles were contraries. Lords *ruled over* other people; slaves, on the contrary, were subject to the rule of others. Yet Jesus is figured for us in *both* roles. Why is that? The answer, surely, is that each metaphor tells us something true—and essential—about Christ, but only as limited or qualified or (as I have put it) disarmed by the other. Jesus is not your ordinary domineering Lord, nor is he your ordinary powerless slave: he is the one who rightly rules in our hearts as Lord because he made himself a slave for our sakes. And the point is that you cannot have the one metaphor without the other. It takes more than one way of talking to intimate the glory of Christ in the saving power of his death on the cross.

My point, then, is that this tactic of disarming is essential to the project of making liturgical language inclusive. We cannot, and in my view should not, always be noncommittal, even if (as I judge) we would do well to be so more often. If we simply surrender words like "Father" and "Lord"—and with them their equally concrete, salty, and vivid disarmers—what we will achieve is a liturgical idiom rather like that of an in-house Pentagon memo: bland, abstract, sexless, mechanical—and, I might add, artificial. What is needed—and here I return to an earlier point—is more inclusion; but in the case of God, what this means is more disarming, since in the case of God male and female are not separable, just as electricity both runs *and* flows. If we are to come to some distant apprehension of the God in whose embrace *all things* "live and move and have their being," we need to picture God as a Father indeed, but a Father who sometimes looks strangely like a Mother, just as we have a Lord indeed, but a Lord who looks strangely like a Servant.

5

But what license is there for such a policy of inclusion? Or, to put it more concretely, for letting, as it were, the feminine *show* in our liturgical and devotional language? I have already alluded to the fact that there is ground for such a policy in the scriptures, even though the scriptures were products of a society that we have learned to call "patriarchal." We do not notice, for example, that the "wisdom" who "is vindicated by her deeds" (Matt. 11:19) is roughly identified in Matthew's Gospel with "the Son of Man" who "came eating and drinking." Wisdom in the traditions on which New Testament writers drew was a feminine figure, of whom it was said that "she is a reflection of eternal light, a spotless mirror of the working of God, and an image of his goodness" (Wis. 7:26); yet various writers in the New Testament characterize

Christ as God's Wisdom (1 Cor. 1:24) or in terms that are virtual quotations from descriptions of Wisdom.[2] This did not seem strange to them or to later Christian teachers. Thus Origen, in his *Commentary on John*, speaks of Wisdom and says that "God entrusted to her the task of furnishing, to the things that exist and to matter, their formation and their forms," and then tells us, in his next breath, that of course this "her" is "the Son of God."[3] That is what I call "disarming"; but of course Origen talks this way without any self-consciousness, just as easily as we talk about electricity running *and* flowing.

Now I should like to go on in this fashion and quote you some bits of Clement of Alexandria, or show you Augustine—not a notorious feminist, I am told—describing the Word of God as a breast, full of superabundant riches, to which he opens his mouth.[4] But all that sort of thing is just *usage*, and the question is *why* such usage is legitimate. So instead I call your attention to some reflective words of one of the architects of the classical doctrine of the Trinity, St. Gregory of Nyssa. Discussing a text from the Song of Songs in which there is a reference to the "mother" of the Bridegroom, that is, of Christ, he writes:

> No one who has given thought to the way we talk about God is going to be agitated about the connotation of the name—that *mother* is mentioned instead of *father*—since the same meaning will be gathered from either term. For since the Deity is neither male nor female—how after all could any such thing be thought of in the case of the Deity, when this [condition of being male or female] is not permanent even for us human beings, but when we all become one in Christ we put off the signs of this difference along with the whole of the old humanity?—for this reason, every name we invent is of the same adequacy for purposes of indicating the divine Nature, since neither *male*

nor *female* defiles the meaning of the inviolate
Nature.[5]

Gregory repeats this point in other places, but the thing for us
to notice is the reason he gives for his position. Gregory believes
that the polarity of male and female is resolved "in Christ"—that
"in Christ," males will discover their femininity and females, their
masculinity; and he further believes, partly on this ground, that
this polarity *cannot* ultimately characterize God, whose unfath-
omable being and goodness transcend any such distinctions. We
may quite properly call God "Father," then, but only in the recognition that God is far more than that, and the same goes for
"Mother." Neither word "defiles...the inviolate Nature"; but—and
this is the crucial point—neither is adequate to it, save perhaps for
certain particular purposes. In another place altogether—in fact, in
one of his treatises against the Arian Eunomius—Gregory explains
his point in other terms. He likens the language and ideas we use
to conceive or to picture God to the tent that Abraham and Sarah
used as they journeyed from Ur of the Chaldees to the land of
God's promise.[6] Like that tent, he says, our ways of talking and
thinking about God are equipment for pilgrims. They are not
what we arrive at, but things that we need and use on the way.
Tents are no doubt very important; it is crucial that the poles and
the cords be strong, and the skins—or perhaps we should say "the
canvas"—sound. No one wants a tent that will blow down at the
first hint of a breeze or one that leaks water in every springtime
rain. But for all that, when the journey is over, the tents will be
dispensed with. They will get us there, but they cannot contain
"the glory that shall be revealed."

He invites us, then, to a degree of *reverence* for God that will
demand on our part something of a new policy where theological
and liturgical language is concerned. Such a policy will mix up elements of the noncommittal (to express our sense of God's universal indwelling of the creation), of the inclusive (to express our
sense of the superabundance of God's being), and of the disarming
(to express our recognition that the God who raised Jesus Christ

the dead is no domesticable idol to be pinned down permanently by any words of ours). And what I like about these liturgies is that they seem instinctively to operate on some such policy as this: they are not trying to rule things out, but to rule things in. Whether they do this job satisfactorily and successfully is, of course, another issue. Probably they do not. But all that means is that we still have work to do, argument to engage in, cudgeling of our imaginations to foster, in the hope that the tent we rely on for our travels will be sound and strong.

Notes

1. Earlier versions of this address were delivered at a New York diocesan Clergy Retreat in 1988, and then to representative clergy and laity of the Diocese of New York, 11 November 1989.

2. See, for example, John 1:1-14; Hebrews 1:2-3; Colossians 1:15-17.

3. See *Commentary on John* I.115-116 (ed. Cécile Blanc, *Sources Chrétiennes* 120 [Paris: Les Editions du Cerf, 1966], I:122).

4. See *Confessions* IX.10 ("Sed inhiabamus ore cordis in superna fluentis fontis tui..."). See below, pp. 44-45, 49, for further discussion of this imagery.

5. Gregory of Nyssa, *Homily VI on the Song of Songs,* in W. Jaeger, ed., *Gregorii Nysseni Opera* (Leiden: Brill, 1960ff.), VI:212-213.

6. W. Jaeger, ed., *Gregorii Nysseni Opera* I:253 (= J.P. Migne, *Patrologia Graeca* 45:940D). English version in *Nicene and Post-Nicene Fathers,* Series 2, Vol V:259.

"Lord, Teach Us to Pray": Historical and Theological Perspectives on Expanding Liturgical Language

Paula S. Datsko Barker

> But you, too, good Jesus, are you not also a
> Mother? Is he not a mother who like a hen gathers
> his chicks beneath his wings? Truly, Lord, you are a
> mother too.[1]

So prayed Anselm of Canterbury, who may have been the most influential theologian ever to set pen to paper on British soil. With this prayer from the eleventh century, we encounter a rich medieval devotional tradition, building on scriptural and patristic antecedents, that employs feminine imagery to facilitate worship of God.

Having observed this tradition, we no longer may dismiss the desire to apply feminine images to God as an inappropriate whim of modern feminists. No longer may we debate whether using such language in worship is a possibility. It is an historical reality. The quest opens before us to discern how these older devotional traditions might inform our present search for effective liturgical language that employs a broader range of imagery for God. I propose to navigate this quest first by surveying some types of feminine images for God that recur in traditional Christian literature. Then we may advance to an exploration of some theological principles which have guided the use of such images in the past and might guide our own experiments in expanding the lexicon of liturgical expression available to Christians in the Episcopal Church.

Traditional Feminine Images of God

Of the feminine images attributed to God in Judeo-Christian communities, holy Wisdom is the oldest and serves as a foundation for the others.[2] Wisdom developed as a specifically female persona in Jewish tradition from the period after the exile to her height of importance during the centuries immediately surrounding the birth of Christ. In the enduring forms of Judaism and Christianity which emerged from these centuries, holy Wisdom became a central theological figure. Having begun as a persona associated with creation, she was adapted by diverse religious groups to respond to their particular concerns. For the wisdom teachers, she came to exemplify learning, piety, and justice. For the prophets, she was the spirit of God who inspires truth. Among the apocalyptic preachers of the Roman occupation, she was the rejected mother of the murdered messengers of God. Bearing these and other associations, she became a figure who connected diverse religious groups. In each adaptation, she represented the desire and means for communion between the divine and humans.

It was mainly through Philo that the Jewish concept of Wisdom (Sophia) became identified with the Platonic concept of the divine Mind (Nous)—containing the forms of all created things—and with the Stoic concept of the Word (Logos). In this transaction, Wisdom's feminine quality usually was repressed.[3] She emerged as a male hypostasis, the Logos, while retaining the divine functions of her earlier persona.[4] This masculinized figure appears at the opening of the Gospel of John: "In the beginning was the Word, and the Word was with God, and the Word was God" (Jn. 1:1).

But the feminine source reappears intermittently.[5] For example, Origen, in his third-century theological treatise *On First Principles*, commences his chapter "On Christ" with a description of the Son of God as God's Wisdom, referred to in feminine grammatical forms. He argues that "the only-begotten Son of God is His wisdom hypostatically existing," that "she contained within herself either the beginnings, or forms, or species of all creation," and consequently "must we understand her to be the Word of God."[6] As warrants, he cites not only Solomon's expressions regarding Wisdom but also the prologue to John's Gospel and the letters of Paul. In the First Letter to the Corinthians, Paul had identified Christ as "the wisdom of God" (I Cor. 1:24). And the eloquent Christological hymn in Colossians 1:15-17, extolling Christ as "the image of the invisible God, the first-born of all creation," echoed Jewish hymns to divine Wisdom.[7]

The identification of Christ with divine Wisdom can be traced at least to the Q material which informed the Gospels of Matthew and Luke, and probably to Jesus himself.[8] In Luke 11:49, Jesus portrays himself as the last of a long line of messengers sent by Wisdom to be rejected and killed by unrepentant generations. In Matthew 23:34, Jesus identifies himself as the one who sent the prophets that have been rejected. In both Gospels, these speeches culminate with Jesus' lament, expressed in an unmistakably maternal image: "Jerusalem, Jerusalem, the city that kills the prophets and stones those who are sent to it! How often have I desired to gather your children together as a hen gathers her brood under her wings, and you were not willing!" (Mt. 23:37-39; Lk. 13:34-35)

Similar connections with Wisdom literature can be observed in Jesus' invitation:

> Come to me, all you that are weary and are carrying heavy burdens, and I will give you rest. Take my yoke upon you, and learn from me; for I am gentle and humble in heart, and you will find rest for your souls. For my yoke is easy, and my burden is light. (Mt. 11:28-30)

Wisdom had beckoned in Proverbs 9:5-6: "Come, eat of my bread and drink of the wine I have mixed. Lay aside immaturity, and live, and walk in the way of insight." And in Sirach 24:19, she had declared: "Come to me, you who desire me, and eat your fill of my fruits." Sirach advised: "Put your feet into [wisdom's] fetters and your neck into her collar.... [A]t last you will find the rest she gives, and she will be changed into joy for you." (Sir. 6:24, 28)

Yet another saying of Jesus' which echoes words from Wisdom is found in John 14:6: "I am the way, and the truth, and the life." Wisdom had proclaimed: "In me is all the grace of the way and the truth...all hope of life" (Sir. 24:25, Vulgate). Given the pervasiveness of Wisdom traditions in Jewish thinking during the life of Christ, one could conclude that those who heard Jesus would have appreciated the implications of his association of himself with divine Wisdom.

In the devotional literature of the Middle Ages, this association of Christ with holy Wisdom continued to develop. Alcuin of York, who orchestrated the renaissance of learning at the court of Charlemagne in the late eighth century, composed a Mass of Holy Wisdom which, having become incorporated into the missal, was used widely until 1570.[9] Hildegard of Bingen, in the twelfth century, emphasized the creative and redemptive action of God through the interchangeable female personas of Wisdom and Charity.[10] Henry Suso, a fourteenth-century German mystic, merged the female figure of Wisdom with the male figure of the crucified Christ. He dedicated himself to the service of both under the single name of Eternal Wisdom. In his *Little Book of Eternal Wisdom*, he asked Lady Wisdom for knowledge of her, and she responded by depicting both the creation of the world and the ministry of Christ. She showed herself in a tree which was revealed as the cross. She also appeared on an altar as a sacramental presence of Christ in feminine form.[11] A popular devotion of "Hours of Eternal Wisdom" developed under Suso's influence. It received further stimulation through the production of a book of hours on this theme by Geert Groote, founder of the late medieval "modern devotion."

Evidence of devotion to Christ as divine Wisdom also can be found in medieval arts. A type of wood sculpture from the Romanesque period known as the "Throne of Wisdom" depicts

Mary seated as an austerely grand figure, providing her lap as the throne for the holy child. The inscription explains, "In the lap of the Mother dwells the Wisdom of the Father."[12] As another example, consider this description, by the artist, of a painting from the fifteenth century:

> Here at the beginning...is Lady Wisdom in the form and figure of a woman, signifying Jesus our Savior, who is called the power and wisdom of God the Father; she is seated on a throne of majesty as true God. And in her right hand she holds a book, and in her left, the world, signifying that through her and from her have come all the knowledge and wisdom by which the world is governed and restored.[13]

Like every powerful symbol of religious devotion, the feminine image of divine Wisdom has been refracted in a multitude of directions, informing clusters of related symbols. Elements of her appear in devotions to Mary, the Mother of God; Holy Mother Church as the bride of God; the mystical marriage of love between Christ and the soul; Charity, mother of the virtues; Lady Philosophy from whom the liberal arts are born; and the goddess Nature, who governs creation and fertility. Each of these manifestations developed rich traditions of its own. And implications from these traditions reflect back onto the continually evolving identification of Jesus Christ in maternal terms.

One frequently used maternal image of Christ refers to him as a nursing mother. The rudiments of this image appear in the second century not only in the Greek of Clement of Alexandria but also in the Latin of Irenaeus, who explained:

> Therefore it was that He, who was the perfect bread of the Father, offered Himself to us as milk, [because we were] as infants. He did this when He appeared as a man, that we, being nourished, as it were, from the breast of His flesh, and having, by

such a course of milk-nourishment, become accustomed to eat and drink the Word of God, may be
able also to contain in ourselves the Bread of
immortality, which is the Spirit of the Father.[14]

One thousand years later, Cistercians like St. Bernard of Clairvaux
and William of St. Thierry employed this image to refer to the
imbibing of divine Wisdom. In a letter to a struggling novice,
Bernard advised, "suck not the wounds but the breasts of the
Crucified. He will be your mother, and you will be his son."[15]
And William's sermon on the Song of Songs explained, "It is your
breasts, O eternal Wisdom, that nourish the holy infancy of your
little ones...."[16]

Another use of maternal terms for Christ serves to offset fearful
views of God with a nurturing image. Clement of Alexandria
brought out the complementarity between fatherhood and motherhood in the Godhead when he wrote:

And God himself is love; and out of love to us
became feminine. In his ineffable essence He is
Father; in His compassion to us He became
Mother. The Father by loving became feminine;
and the great proof of this is He whom He Begot
of Himself; and the fruit brought forth by love is
love.[17]

Similarly, Augustine, in his treatment of Psalm 101:2, suggested a
complementarity of masculine and feminine aspects patterned on
expected social roles when he wrote, "Christ exercises fatherly
authority and maternal love."[18]

Establishing such complementarity in the Godhead was the
principal role that Jesus as Mother played in Julian of Norwich's
theology.[19] Souls oppressed by dreadful fear of the awful majesty
of God could be persuaded of God's accessibility by means of the
image of divine motherhood:

But often when our falling and our wretchedness
are shown to us, we are so much afraid and so

> greatly ashamed of ourselves that we scarcely know
> where we can put ourselves. But then our courteous
> Mother does not wish us to fall away....(Instead, we
> should) behave like a child. For when it is distressed
> and frightened, it runs quickly to its mother; and if
> it can do no more, it calls to the mother for help
> with all its might.[20]

The image of divine motherhood promotes in the believer the disposition of childlike trust that is the essential basis for spiritual life.

Bernard expanded the relevance of this image by employing it not only devotionally but also as a model for ecclesiastical leadership.[21] He wrote of his relationship with a monk from his charge who had moved away to become head of another abbey, "I am the mother and he the son....A mother cannot forget the child she bore, and the grief I feel for him proclaims him to be my son."[22] Bernard exhorted other abbots to conform to this maternal model: "to let your bosoms expand with milk, not swell with passion"; to be like "mothers, not masters."[23]

Another way of viewing Jesus' motherhood discerns in Jesus' death a birthing of the children of God into new life. Drawing upon the image of all creation groaning in travail presented by Paul in Romans 8:22, the labor pangs of a new creation are attached to the devotional figure of Christ crucified. Julian made this connection by juxtaposing her vision of Mary as an obedient soul with a vision of Christ on the cross:

> So our Lady is our mother, in whom we are all
> enclosed and born of her in Christ, for she who is
> mother of our savior is mother of all who are saved
> in our savior; and our savior is our true Mother, in
> whom we are endlessly born and out of whom we
> shall never come.[24]

The most stunning example of this type of imagery occurs, however, in the meditations of Marguerite d'Oignt, a Carthusian prioress of the late thirteenth century:

Ah, who has seen a woman give birth thus! And when the hour of birth came, they placed You on the bed of the Cross. And it is not astonishing your veins ruptured, as you gave birth in one single day to the whole world.[25]

Having observed even this small sample of historical devotional language employing feminine images for God, many modern Christians are amazed by the ease with which their ancient counterparts blended feminine and masculine attributions in their worship. Our minds balk at the possibility of leaping the seemingly insurmountable chasm that gender represents. Our predecessors, however, seem not to have noticed this obstacle, or at least not to have projected the significance onto it that we do.

One explanation for this difference in perspective relates to the structure of the English language. Unlike languages such as French and German, English does not assign grammatical gender to its nouns. Since the noun for "giraffe" is feminine in French, Parisians find no incongruity in referring to a male giraffe by using a feminine pronoun. English-speaking students of French find this discrepancy confusing, if not amusing. English assumes that the application of a gendered pronoun corresponds to the biological sex of the object. Thus the exclusive use of male terms for God carries a more distorting effect in English than in many other languages.

Theological Principles Sustaining These Images

To come to terms with the images we have just encountered, we must refer first to the fundamental theological principle that human understanding is limited, as is the language in which theological insight and devotional intention might be expressed. We are creatures, conditioned into prejudices by our historical situations; and we are sinners, accustomed to manipulating those prejudices for our personal advantage in opposition to the charitable designs of God. As creatures and sinners who have been redeemed, we confess the finitude and self-centeredness that still confine us. So Paul said, "Now we see in a mirror, dimly...." (I Cor. 13:12). After almost two thousand years of fervent theological activity, his statement still describes the best that human understanding can achieve. From the tension between our recognition of this condition and the concomitant extension of divine grace toward us that calls forth a loving response, our language of worship emerges. From this same tension flows also our desire continually to refine and reform the terms of our prayer.

Thus theological language has been understood historically to have both a positive and a negative aspect. Positively, we name God and describe God's attributes in words familiar to human experience: "God is good," "God is wise," "God is judge," "God is father," "God is maternal," "God is a fiery presence." Some of these attributions carry more weight than others; those with scriptural sources are endowed with the greatest authority. Whether they are styled as metaphors or similes or any other form of speech, they convey truths about God—truths that are always inescapably partial.

The negative aspect of theological language serves to remind us of our limits and to stretch our imaginations into the mystery of the divine. Whatever we might say positively about God is more truly said negatively. For example, God is "good," but more precisely God is "not good" in the sense that God exceeds our finite concepts of goodness: God is "more than good." The anonymous writer known as Dionysius the Areopagite articulated this principle in a text which has been a foundational source for both the Western and the Eastern Christian theological traditions. He insisted that God's divinity ultimately:

> ...is not sonship or fatherhood and is nothing known to us or to any other being....There is no speaking of it, nor name nor knowledge of it....for it is both beyond every assertion, being the perfect and unique cause of all things, and, by virtue of its

preeminently simple and absolute nature, free of
every limitation, beyond every limitation; it is also
beyond every denial.[26]

Application of this negative principle in theological language serves
as a guard against idolatry.

In devotional language, juxtaposition of diverse images for God
can serve a similar function. As John of Damascus explained:

Inasmuch, then, as He is incomprehensible, He is
also unnameable. But inasmuch as He is the cause
of all and contains in Himself the reasons and
causes of all that is, He receives names drawn from
all that is, even from opposites: for example, He is
called light and darkness, water and fire: in order
that we may know that these are not of His essence
but that He is supraessential and unnameable; but
inasmuch as He is the cause of all, He receives
names from all His effects....These, then, are the
affirmations and the negations, but the sweetest
names are a combination of both: for example, the
supraessential Essence, the Godhead that is more
than God, the Beginning that is above beginning,
and such like.[27]

We might add other examples of incongruous language. Clement
of Alexandria stated: "to those babes that seek the Word, the
Father's breasts of love supply milk."[28] Ambrose declared of
Christ: "He is, then, the Virgin Who was espoused, the Virgin
Who bare us, Who fed us with her own milk...."[29] And Julian
used masculine pronouns to refer to Jesus as Mother.[30]
Multiplication of images for God and dissonance in the conjunction of them can provoke insight by drawing our understanding
beyond conventionality into mystery.

Is the language of the scriptures and the creeds somehow
exempt from the limitations otherwise recognized in human discourse about God? Though they function regulatively in Christian

communions like our own, these sources do not escape the consequences of human finitude. Scripture is revelation from God, yet it is conveyed in such language as humans can perceive.[31] If such words were possible by which God could convey the fullness of the divine majesty and benevolence, they would be beyond our human vocabulary and would exceed our comprehension. The words of scripture, like the incarnation itself, are acts of condescension on God's part by which the divine enters into the limiting conditions of human history. Through condescension, God draws us into relationship with the divine such that we might experientially know at least some part of that which is rationally and verbally incomprehensible. Thus the limits of human nature, fallen and redeemed, are expanded by the operations of grace.

The creeds exist because of the limitations inherent in scriptural language. Diverse communities, employing the same scriptures, devised divergent belief systems and ritual practices. Adherence to an historical creed serves as a sign of affiliation among similar communities and as a regulative tool for the faith of future generations. Creeds function as "signposts against heresy," according to Athanasius. They function normatively as paradigms to uphold a particular facet of divine mystery under contention. Nevertheless, the terms they employ are historically and linguistically conditioned. As Augustine recognized in his treatise *On the Trinity*, the Greeks' and Latins' terms for the unity and distinctions of the Trinity originally sounded incorrect to each other when translated literally.[32]

Does the Nicene Creed's use of the words Father, Son, and Spirit to name the persons of the Trinity exclude the possibility of employing feminine designations for the divine? Historically, the Nicene Creed emerged from a struggle between Orthodox and Arian Christians primarily over the eternal preexistence versus the createdness of the second person of the Trinity. In this debate, both sides referred to scriptural texts about the feminine persona of Wisdom to defend their convictions about the Son.[33] Wisdom's feminine quality was not under contention, and her identification with the Son was accepted.

The Nicene Creed does not employ the terms Father and Son to exclude forever feminine designations for the Trinity by establishing God's masculine gender. Rather, these terms articulate paradigmatically the mystery of unity, relationality, and personhood in God which Christians confess.[34] Augustine attempted to articulate new variations of the paradigm through his relational and psychological analogies.[35] Julian set forth interlocking triads of images for God to describe the relationships in the Trinity and their roles in human salvation.[36] By these means they hoped to come to understand and to love more fully what they already believed by faith.

The motives of contemporary theologians who attempt to expand our doxological lexicon may be interpreted similarly. Creedal forms and scriptural terms must be honored as traditional paradigmatic expressions: the patterns they instantiate should be recognizable in contemporary adaptions. Neglected devotional themes from earlier periods of church history may be employed today not only as elements to be retrieved for current liturgical use but, perhaps more importantly, as illustrations of the methods by which our ancestors in the faith attempted to expand and adapt traditional images of God.

Underlying the current debates in the Episcopal Church over the viability of expanding our images for God are fundamental concerns about the unity and diversity of our church. Yet the possibility of unity in multiplicity is precisely what the doctrine of the Trinity reveals. Rather than using the language of this doctrine to splinter and divide, let us open ourselves, in our praying, to the work of the triune God among us, that we might be empowered to reflect the mystery of divine community into the world.

Notes

1. Anselm, Prayer 10 to St. Paul, *The Prayers and Meditations of St. Anselm*, trans. Sr. Benedicta Ward (Harmondsworth, 1973), p. 154 (*Orationes* 65, in J.P. Migne, ed., *Patrologiae Cursus Completus: Series Latina*, 221 vols. [Paris, 1841-1864] 158:981 [hereafter cited as *PL*]). Compare also Augustine's use of this image in *Questionum Evangeliorum* 2.26, in *PL* 35:1330; and *Enarratio in Psalmum* 90, in *PL* 37:1160-61.

2. I am indebted to Barbara Newman's illuminating work on the development of Wisdom/Sophia in Christian tradition. See especially "The Pilgrimage of Christ-Sophia," *Vox Benedictina* 9 (1992): 9-37; and "Some Medieval Theologians and the Sophia Tradition," *The Downside Review* 108 (1990): 111-30.

3. One of the exceptions is in Philo's *Questiones et Solutiones in Genesis* 4:97: "Who is to be considered the daughter of God but Wisdom who is the first-born mother of all things and most of all of those who are greatly purified in soul?"

4. See Philo, *De fuga et inventione* 51-52.

5. Other examples would include Hilary of Poitiers, *Commentarium in Matthaeum* 10, in *PL* 9:982; Jerome, *Commentarium in Evangelicum Matthaei*, in *PL* 26:181.

6. Origen, *On First Principles* I.ii.2-3, in Alexander Roberts and James Donaldson, eds., *The Ante-Nicene Fathers*, 10 vols. (Grand Rapids, Mich., 1951-53), 4:246 (hereafter cited as *ANF*) (*Patrologiae Cursus Completus: Series Graeca*, 161 vols. [Paris, 1857-66], 11:130-32 [hereafter cited as *PG*]).

7. See further in R. S. Barbour, "Creation, Wisdom, and Christ," in *Christ the Lord*, ed. Harold Rowdon (Edinburgh, 1976), pp. 22-42; Elizabeth Schüssler, "Wisdom Mythology and the Christological Hymns of the New Testament," in *Aspects of Wisdom of Judaism and Early Christianity*, ed. Robert L. Wilken (Notre Dame, 1975), pp. 17-41.

8. See further in Felix Christ, *Jesus Sophia: Die Sophia-Christologie bei den Synoptikern* (Zurich, 1970); Richard Edwards, *A Theology of Q: Eschatology, Prophecy, and Wisdom* (Philadelphia, 1976); Ronald Piper, *Wisdom in the Q-Tradition* (Cambridge, 1989).

9. Alcuin, *Missa de sancta sapientia*, in *PL* 101:450-1.

10. See Newman, "Some Medieval Theologians," pp. 118-22. For a more comprehensive study, see Barbara Newman, *Sister of Wisdom: St. Hildegard's Theology of the Feminine* (Berkeley, 1987).

11. See further in Newman, "Some Medieval Theologians," pp. 122-24.

12. See further in Ilene Forsyth, *The Throne of Wisdom: Wood Sculptures of the Madonna in Romanesque France* (Princeton, 1972), pp. 22-30.

13. Peter R. Monks, *The Brussels Horloge de Sapience* (Leiden, 1990), pp. 134-35.

14. Irenaues, *Against Heresies* IV.38.1, in *ANF* 1:521 (*PG* 7:1105-6); compare also III.24.1, in *ANF* 1:458 (*PG* 7:966-67). On Clement, see n.28 below.

15. Bernard, *The Letters of St. Bernard of Clairvaux*, trans. Bruno Scott James (London, 1953), p. 449, does not give a literal translation. See instead Letter 322 in *PL* 182:527.

16. William of St. Thierry, *Exposition on the Canticle*, chap. 38, in *The Works of William of St. Thierry: Exposition on the Song of Songs*, Cistercian Fathers Series 6 (Spencer, Mass., 1970), p. 30. Other examples of this image can be observed in British writings such as Hugh Farmer, ed., *The Monk of Farne* (Baltimore, 1961), pp. 64, 69; Robert Hugh Benson, ed., *A Book of the Love of Jesus: A Collection of Ancient English Devotions in Prose and Verse* (London, 1904), p. 137; and Aelred of Rievaulx, *De institutione* 26, in *Aelred of Rievaulx 1:*

Treatises and Pastoral Prayers, trans. M. P. McPherson (Spencer, Mass., 1971), p. 73.

17. Clement of Alexandria, *The Salvation of the Rich Man* 37, in *ANF* 2:601 (*PG* 9:641-2).

18. Augustine, *Enarratio in Psalmum* 101:7-8, in *PL* 37:1299.

19. See further in my article, "The Motherhood of God in Julian of Norwich's Theology," *The Downside Review* 100 (1982): 290-304. On the trinitarian structure of her thought, see n.36 below.

20. Julian of Norwich, *Showings*, ed. Edmund Colledge and James Walsh (New York, 1978), long text chap. 61, p. 301 (Julian, *A Book of Showings to the Anchoress Julian of Norwich*, 2 vols. [Toronto, 1978], 2:605-6 [hereafter cited as *BSAJN*).

21. Caroline Walker Bynum analyzes the use of maternal imagery by Bernard and six other Cistercians in "Jesus as Mother and Abbot as Mother," *Jesus as Mother: Studies in the Spirituality of the High Middle Ages* (Berkeley, 1982), pp. 110-69.

22. Bernard, *Letters*, p. 413 (*PL* 182:466).

23. Bernard, Sermon 23.2, in *On the Song of Songs,* trans. Kiliam Walsh, Cistercian Fathers Series 4 (Spencer, Mass., 1971), 2:27 (Bernard of Clairvaux, *Sancti Bernardi Opera*, ed. Jean Leclercq, C. H. Talbot, and Henri Rochais [Rome, 1957-], 1:139-40). Compare also Bernard, Sermon 10.3, in *Song of Songs* 1:62-63 (*Opera*, 1:49-50).

24. Julian, *Showings*, long text ch. 57, p.292 (*BSAJN* 2:580).

25. A. Duraffour, P. Gardette, and P. Durdilly, *Les Oeuvres de Marguerite d'Oignt* (Paris, 1965), pp. 33-36; compare also pp. 31-32.

26. Dionysius the Areopagite, *The Mystical Theology* 5, in *Pseudo-Dionysius: The Complete Works,* trans. Colm Luibheid (New York, 1987), p. 141. Compare Augustine, *On the Trinity* VII.4.7, in Philip Schaff, ed., *A Select Library of the Nicene and Post-Nicene Fathers of the Christian Church* (Grand

Rapids, Mich., 1955-56), 1st ser., 3:109 (hereafter cited as *NPNF*) (*PL* 42:939): "For God is more truly thought than He is uttered, and exists more truly than He is thought."

27. John of Damascus, *On the Orthodox Faith* 1.12, in *NPNF*, 2nd ser., 9:14.

28. Clement of Alexandria, *The Instructor* 1.6, in *ANF* 2:221 (*PG* 8:505-6).

29. Ambrose, *Concerning Virgins* 1.5, in *NPNF*, 2nd ser., 10:366 (*PL* 16:205).

30. For example, "So our Mother works in mercy on all his beloved children who are docile and obedient to him...." Julian, *Showings*, long text chap. 58, p. 294 (*BSAJN* 2:586).

31. Augustine explained that, though God is neither corporeal nor spiritual, scripture uses language referring to corporeal and spiritual things to draw our hearts and minds to the divine (*On the Trinity* I.1.2, in *NPNF*, 1st ser., 3:18 [*PL* 42:821]). Similarly, Calvin, in his discussion of the relationship between scriptural terms and the doctrine of the Trinity, compares scripture's anthropomorphisms to babytalk such as a nanny might use to communicate with a beloved child (John Calvin, *Institutes of the Christian Religion* I.13.i, in *Calvin: Institutes of the Christian Religion*, ed. John McNeill, 2 vols. [Philadelphia, 1960], 1:121).

32. Augustine, *On the Trinity* VII.4.7, in *NPNF*, 1st ser., 3:109 (*PL* 42:939).

33. See Jaroslav Pelikan, *The Emergence of the Catholic Tradition (100-500)* (Chicago, 1971), pp. 186-200.

34. For example, Gregory of Nyssa explains in his treatise *Against Eunomius* II.3 (*NPNF*, 2nd ser., 5:103 [*PG* 45:473-4]): "...for it is plain that the title of Father does not present to us the Essence, but only indicates the relation to the Son." See also *PG* 44:116.

35. Thus he described the Trinity through the relationships

among one that loves, one that is loved, and love; the Mind, the Knowledge by which the Mind knows itself, and the Love by which the Mind loves itself and its Knowledge; and finally Memory, Understanding, and Will (*On the Trinity* VIII-X, in *NPNF*, 1st ser., 3:115-143 [*PL* 42:945-84]).

36. God is Father, Mother, Lord; Power, Wisdom, Love; and source of our nature, mercy, and grace (Julian, *Showings*, long text chaps. 58-59, pp. 293-97 [*BSAJN* 2:582-93]).

A contrasting approach arose among ancient Syriac-speaking Christians. Because the term for the Holy Spirit in semitic languages (*ruach*) has female gender, these Christians identified her with the Wisdom of God, moved her to the second place in the Trinity as the mother of Jesus, and worshipped the triune Father, Mother, and Son. Examples can be found in the *Odes of Solomon*, ed. and trans. J.H. Charlesworth (Missoula, 1977); and in Theophilus of Antioch, *Ad Autolycum*, ed. and trans. Robert Grant (Oxford, 1970).

The Feminine as Omitted, Optional, or Alternative Story: A Review of the Episcopal Eucharistic Lectionary

Jean Campbell, OSH

Scripture, although heavily influenced by patriarchal and hierarchical structure, contains a significant account of women in salvation history and of the understanding of God in feminine as well as masculine images and metaphors. Yet these images, part of the Christian tradition, are largely unknown.

My mother has been a member of the Episcopal Church for over sixty-five years, attending Sunday worship and faithfully reading scripture on a daily basis over much of her lifetime. During a visit she said to me: "I know you're not a heretic but what is it you're doing with inclusive language—where do you find these feminine images of God that you talk about?" I took her Bible and began to read passages from Isaiah 49 and 66. She said: "I've never heard those passages before."

Suddenly I began to put some pieces together. Here is a woman who has been immersed in the lectionaries of the church most of her life yet who had never heard or been invited to reflect upon the fullness of scripture. It was then that I decided to explore the use of scripture in the lectionary of the Episcopal Church.

The ways in which we understand and know God are formed within the liturgy of the church. What we pray and sing as well as the stories we retell in public worship, form and shape what we believe about God and about ourselves in relationship to God and to each other:

> When Christians gather for worship, their identity
> as Christians is established or reinforced: the com-
> mon heritage is recalled and celebrated; their
> heroes, founders, and holy people are commemo-
> rated; and the work of God in human history and
> in the life of the community is recognized.[1]

If we do not know when and by whom the feminine images of
God and the story of women in salvation history are disclosed, we
need to reexamine what stories we tell within our liturgy.

It is my contention that feminine images and stories of women
are to be found in the Bible, but they have been ignored, designated
as optional, or assigned as alternative scripture readings within the
eucharistic lectionary of the Episcopal Church. Feminine images
of God and the stories of faithful women have not been recognized
by those responsible for appointing the lections, as a significant
part of the story of the people of God.

As such, when feminists speak of reclaiming the feminine
aspects of salvation history, the common reaction is that one is
somehow changing either scripture or the tradition. In fact many
feminists are merely asking that the fullness of the scriptures and
tradition be recognized within the public prayer of the church.

This study focuses upon the Sunday eucharistic lectionary of
The Book of Common Prayer and includes the portions of scripture appointed for every Sunday in the three-year cycle along with
those lessons appointed for Christmas and Ascension Day. In those
instances where some verses are optional, they were included in the
readings studied. Where alternative readings are given, all the lections appointed were included in the study.

Marjorie Procter-Smith identifies several levels of interpretation
which are operable when one examines the lectionary. First, the
lectionary is selective: it chooses to use certain texts and exclude
others, and hence it operates on a hermeneutical principle. The
lessons appointed for Sundays imply that they are important to
nourish and sustain the ongoing life of the community. A second

level of interpretation is defining what verses of a given selection shall be read: the lectionary defines the limits of the text, its beginning and end. The third level is the relationship between the first and second lessons and the Gospel reading: how the lessons interact will interpret certain texts.[2]

I would suggest a fourth level of interpretation: where the text is placed in relation to the calendar of the church year. The lectionary is rooted in the cycle of the church year and as such will determine what stories are remembered within significant festal cycles as well as how often a particular passage will be read.

In her article, Marjorie Procter-Smith establishes two categories, "significant" and "peripheral," to designate biblical passages which include references either to feminine images of God or to women. For the purposes of this study, pericopes in which women played a prominent role or the image of God was feminine are regarded as "significant." For example, God as mother, Isaiah 66:13; the woman anointing Jesus, Matthew 26:1-13; the parable of the lost coin, Luke 15:8-10; and wives being subject to their husbands, Ephesians 5:21-33, are identified as "significant" passages. Where there is passing reference to the feminine, these are regarded as peripheral, such as the metaphorical references to Jerusalem, Isaiah 65:18; reference to a hen gathering her brood, Luke 13:34; the "women of our group," Luke 24:22; and "Apphia our sister" in Philemon 2. The categories of significant and peripheral do not judge the text as being negative or positive in reference to females or feminine images of God.[3]

The following chart shows the total number of pericopes included in the study and the percentage of significant and peripheral passages:

	O.T.	Gospel	Epistles	Acts
Total Pericopes	175	182	164	24
Ref. to Women	48 (23%)	47 (21%)	9 (5%)	6 (25%)
(S)	12	23	1	0
(P)	36	24	8	6

There are also six pericopes from the book of Revelation, one of which makes reference to the "bride" (Rev. 22:17). The lessons from Acts are appointed for the Easter season, and in each case alternatives are appointed.

Given the patriarchal nature of scripture, the lections, on the whole, are positive in regard to women and seem to be numerous. However, when one begins to examine the lectionary and the various levels through which the scripture is interpreted one begins to discern a pattern in which the feminine metaphors for God and the experience of women are omitted or are assigned as optional or alternative readings. For instance, of the forty-seven Gospel pericopes eleven passages are designated as optional readings.

For the principle service of Easter, Year A, John 20:1-18 is appointed with verses 11-18 optional. An alternative Gospel, Matthew 28:1-10, is also appointed. The optional verses from John contain the encounter between Mary Magdalene and the risen Lord with her subsequent proclamation to the disciples: "I have seen the Lord." John 20:11-18 is the Gospel appointed for Tuesday in Easter Week in all three years. However, the fact that it is an optional passage in an alternative Gospel reading at the principal service of Easter once every three years will diminish the possibility of the community hearing the story of the appearance of Jesus to Mary Magdalene and her proclamation of the resurrection.[4]

There is an interesting comparison to be found in the reading for Easter Year C where Luke 24:1-10 omits verse 11, which recounts the disbelief of the disciples in response to the women's proclamation that they had experienced the empty tomb and were given a message. To include the Marcan account of the fear of the women (Mark 16:1-8) in Year B but leave out the incredulity of the male disciples in Luke (24:11) causes one to ask what the underlying assumptions were in selecting the verses.

The story of the Samaritan woman at the well is read on Lent 3A. Again the portion of the story which is optional, John 4:27-

38, contains the questioning of the disciples and also relates the woman's evangelism to those in the city to "come and see" (v. 29). Both the amazement that Jesus would be revealed to a woman and her activity in bringing others to Jesus is not considered to be significant enough to be included in the pericope.

The story of the annunciation to Abraham and Sarah (Proper 11C, Gen. 18:1-10a [10b-14]) also provides optional verses. Sarah's response of confusion and laughter to the promise that she would bear a child is contained in the optional verses. The Gospel for this Sunday is the story of Mary and Martha, Luke 10:38-42. The cluster of stories on this Sunday provide a rare opportunity to explore the human encounter with the divine as experienced in the lives of women.

On the Fifth Sunday of Lent Year A, John 11:1-44 is appointed with verses 1-17 as optional. The optional verses identify the relationship of Mary, Martha, and Lazarus with Jesus along with the discussion between Jesus and the disciples of the belief which may be known in the raising of Lazarus. Verse 45, which speaks of those "who had come with Mary," saw and believed, is not included in the lection. There appears to be a pattern, consciously or unconsciously determined, in which the stories of women are considered optional or are omitted in the portions of scripture read in our Sunday worship.

The role of women is also ignored or diminished in the passion Gospels through both omissions and the use of optional passages. The passion Gospel appointed for Palm Sunday, in all cases, provides for portions of the story to be deleted. While the passion Gospel is the longest reading of the church year, the fact remains that those verses which recount the role of women in the salvific mission of Jesus are considered optional by the church. Often on the parochial level, the optional portions are omitted in order to "shorten" the liturgy.

In all three synoptic accounts of the passion appointed for Palm Sunday, the optional passages relate the involvement of women in

the passion of Jesus. In the Matthean account, the following verses
are optional:

> Many women were also there, looking on from a
> distance; they had followed Jesus from Galilee and
> had provided for him. Among them were Mary
> Magdalene, and Mary the mother of James and
> Joseph, and the mother of the sons of Zebedee.
> (Matt. 27:55-56)

The remaining verses, Matt. 27:57-66, also optional, recount the
burial of Jesus and the watchfulness of Mary Magdalene and the
other Mary at the sepulcher after Joseph of Arimathea had left.

The Marcan account of the passion, appointed for Year B,
allows for the omission of Mark 15:40-47. Again, this is the
account of the women who followed, provided for Jesus, and saw
where he was laid in the tomb.

Year C (Luke [22:39-71], 23:1-49 [50-56]) does include Luke
23:49 which states that the women who were with Jesus from
Galilee "stood at a distance, watching these things." However, the
optional passage, Luke 23:50-56, recounts the ministry of the
women who followed, saw the tomb, and prepared spices and oint-
ments for the burial of Jesus.

The ministry of women is found at the beginning and the end
of the passion narratives in both Matthew and Mark. Yet the stories of the woman anointing the feet of Jesus at Bethany, Matthew
26:6-13 and Mark 14:3-9, are omitted from the Sunday eucharistic lectionary.

Mark 14:3-9 is separated from the passion narrative and
appointed for Monday in Holy Week as an alternative to the
Johannine account of the anointing of Jesus' feet by Mary of
Bethany (John 12:1-11). The Johannine account shifts the emphasis from the service of the woman to the dialogue between Judas
and Jesus and the concern for the poor. Matthew 26:1-5, 14-25 is
appointed as an alternative reading for Wednesday in Holy Week,
but this omits the anointing of the feet of Jesus at the house of

Simon the leper. One must ask why the one Gospel story identified as the one to be remembered wherever the Gospel is preached, should be deleted from the Sunday lectionary. The church of the twentieth century obviously has experienced a shift from the first - century evangelists in what is considered appropriate for proclamation within the eucharistic assembly. Matthew states: "Truly I tell you, wherever this good news is proclaimed in the whole world, what she has done will be told in remembrance of her" (Matt. 26:13); again in the Gospel of Mark: "...wherever the good news is proclaimed in the whole world, what she has done will be told in remembrance of her" (Mk. 14:9).

The compilers of the lectionary did include the story of the woman anointing the feet of Jesus in the Gospel of Luke. Luke 7:36-50 is appointed for Proper 6C. Luke does not include it as part of the passion narrative but places it earlier in the Gospel. There are some notable differences in the story as recounted by Luke in comparison with the story in either Matthew or Mark. In Luke, the focus is on forgiveness and the teaching to Simon. Only in Luke is the woman identified as a sinner: "And a woman in the city, who was a sinner" (Lk. 7:37). The first lesson appointed with this Gospel is II Samuel 11:26-12:10,13-15, the story of Nathan's confrontation with David who had slept with the "wife of Uriah." The sin of David and the woman who is a sinner are paralleled in the selection of the propers for this day. The fullness of the faithful witness of the woman anointing the feet of Jesus is thus further diminished.

It should be further noted that the lectionary of The Book of Common Prayer omits the verses which follow the Lucan story of the woman anointing the feet of Jesus: Luke 8:1-3. In this pericope about discipleship, the twelve are said to be with Jesus in his preaching, "as well as some women who had been cured...: Mary, called Magdalene,...and Joanna,...and Susanna, and many others, who provided for them out of their resources." The women who had been healed followed and provided support for the ministry of Jesus and the disciples.[5]

The story of the Shunammite woman and Elisha, II Kings 4:(8-17) 18-21 (22-31) 32-37, is appointed for the Fifth Sunday after the Epiphany in Year B. The optional passages tell the story of the recognition, hospitality, persistence and assertiveness of the Shunammite woman: she is a wealthy woman who offers Elisha hospitality (v. 8); "I am sure that this man...is a holy man of God" (v. 9). She asks for nothing in return, yet Elisha promises her a child because she has none and her husband is old. In verses 22-25 she is certain that the man of God can help her son who is ill, and she is the one who takes the initiative and seeks out Elisha. This is a story of a woman who is strong, perceptive, and faithful, but again, those portions which portray the fullness of the woman's faithfulness are optional. The lectionary links this story with the healing of Simon's mother-in-law (Mark 1:29-39), which emphasizes the healing aspect of the story.

Another omission from the proclamation of the story of salvation is the woman with the issue of blood. The story of Jairus' daughter and the woman who has faith are intricately interwoven stories in the synoptic Gospels. Yet when they are appointed for proclamation in the Sunday liturgy there is a curious twist: only the Marcan story of Jairus' daughter is told (Mark 5:22-24, 35b-43; Proper 8B), and the faithfulness of the woman "suffering from hemorrhages" (Mk. 5:25-34) is omitted from the proclamation of this Marcan account to the community. The parallel stories, Matthew 9:18-26 and Luke 8:40-56, are not included in the eucharistic lectionary.[6]

In reviewing the lections, one begins to notice that some of the most prominent feminine passages in scripture fall on days which can be replaced with other propers. A major attempt was made in the calendar of the church year to maintain the primacy of Sunday, yet if a feast day falls on a Sunday, "when desired...the Collect, Preface, and one or more of the Lessons appointed" for feasts of our Lord and all other major feasts may be used instead of the Sunday propers, except on Sundays "from the Last Sunday after

Pentecost through the First Sunday after the Epiphany, or from the Last Sunday after the Epiphany through Trinity Sunday."[7]

The only passage in the Gospels which provides a feminine metaphor for God is the story of the woman with the lost coin in Luke 15:1-10, appointed for Proper 19C. Proper 19 falls on the Sunday closest to September fourteenth, Holy Cross Day, a feast of our Lord. Therefore, when Holy Cross Day falls on a Sunday, "when desired" the propers for Holy Cross Day can be substituted for those appointed. Some parishes, contrary to the rubrics of the BCP, continue to transfer a major feast to a Sunday, thus further diluting the Sunday lectionary.[8] The woman with the lost coin is a complementary story to the parable of the shepherd with the lost sheep in Luke. It will be read once every three years, if it is not supplanted by the festal propers.

Another explicit feminine metaphor for God, Isaiah 66:10-16, occurs in Proper 9 of Year C on the Sunday closest to July sixth, hence on the Sunday closest to Independence Day, a day listed as a major feast.[9] A number of parishes use the propers appointed for July fourth instead of the Sunday propers appointed. In the practice of many parishes, one questions how often people will hear:

> I will extend prosperity to her like a river, and the
> wealth of the nations like an overflowing stream;
> and you shall nurse and be carried on her arm, and
> dandled on her knees. As a mother comforts her
> child, so I will comfort you; you shall be comforted
> in Jerusalem. (Is. 66:12-13)

Isaiah 49:8-18, containing the passage: "Can a woman forget her nursing child, or show no compassion for the child of her womb? Even these may forget, yet I will not forget you" (v. 15), is appointed for the Eighth Sunday after the Epiphany in Year A and also for Proper 3A. One might assume that in a forty-year period, one will hear a given proper twelve times or more. Yet the Fourth through Ninth Sundays after the Epiphany and Propers 1-4 are dependent upon the movable date of Easter. From 1985 to 2025, this passage will be read five times on the Eighth Sunday after the Epiphany in Year A, and as Proper 3A once, a total of six times in forty years.[10]

This paper has not attempted to include an extensive account of the omissions of the stories of women in salvation history or to provide an exhaustive list of the feminine images of God contained in the scriptures. Noticeably absent from the lectionary are selections from the books of Ruth, Judith, Esther, and Judges, along with maternal metaphors from the Old Testament such as Deuteronomy 32:18 and Psalm 131. The Acts of the Apostles and the Epistles recount the stories of women, such as Lydia, Tabitha and Priscilla, who supported and sustained the missionary activities of Peter and Paul. Yet these too are excluded from the public retelling of the story of the church.

I have focused on the Sunday eucharistic lectionary of The Book of Common Prayer and how the scriptures appointed are used in the parochial setting. I have shown that those stories which are included are all too often designated as optional, appointed as an alternative text, or displaced by the cycle of feasts. We do not know the stories of women contained in scripture nor are we aware of the rich feminine metaphors for God in Hebrew Scripture because they have not been part of the story proclaimed within our Sunday eucharistic worship. The fullness of the compassionate, merciful, and loving God as well as the history of women who have been faithful have not been considered of value to be heard publicly in the gathering of the community of faith.

Many of the issues raised in this paper have been addressed by the work of the ecumenical Consultation on Common Texts with the publication of the *Revised Common Lectionary*. The place of women in the lectionary was one of five areas of critique of the *Common Lectionary*, and consequently the task force which prepared the *Revised Common Lectionary* worked consciously to make more evident the role of women in the biblical story.[11]

I believe that the time has come for serious consideration of working on the Episcopal eucharistic lectionary so that what is proclaimed will begin to allow the fullness of the biblical story to be told. The church needs to revise the lectionary so that the story of the whole people of God may be proclaimed in the Body of Christ.

Notes

1. Marjorie Procter-Smith, "Images of Women in the Lectionary," in *Women Invisible in Church and Theology*, ed. Elizabeth Schüssler Fiorenza and Mary Collins, *Concilium* Vol. 182 (Edinburgh: T. & T. Clark, 1985), p. 51.

2. Ibid., p. 52.

3. Ibid., pp. 54-55.

4. The *Revised Common Lectionary* has John 20:1-18 as the first option for the principal Easter reading in all three years, with synoptic lections as alternatives (Consultation on Common Texts, *Revised Common Lectionary* [Nashville: Abingdon, 1992], pp. 31, 48, 63).

   The *Revised Common Lectionary* is the work of the ecumenical Consultation on Common Texts (CCT). The Episcopal Church is a participant in the CCT, and a representative from the Episcopal Church served on the task force that prepared the *Revised Common Lectionary.*

5. The *Revised Common Lectionary* (p. 66) appoints Luke 7:36-8:3 as the Gospel for Proper 6C.

6. The *Revised Common Lectionary* (p. 50) includes the full pericope, Mark 5:21-43. The *Revised Common Lectionary* (p. 34) also includes the Matthean account as the Gospel appointed for Proper 5A, where the pericope recounting the healing of Jairus' daughter and the woman with the issue of blood is linked with the story of the calling of Matthew.

7. BCP 1979, p. 16.

8. *The Living Church*, Sept. 12, 1993, contained a letter to the editor requesting such a use of holy days on Sundays with specific reference to Holy Cross Day.

9. BCP 1979, p. 16.

10. Computations made from "Tables for Finding Holy Days," BCP 1979, pp. 880-85.

11. *Revised Common Lectionary*, pp. 77-78. On the Consultation on Common Texts, see above, note 4.

A THEOLOGICAL CONSULTATION ON LANGUAGE AND LITURGY

Seabury-Western Theological Seminary
Evanston, Illinois

September 9—11, 1993

Introduction:
A Theological Consultation on
Language and Liturgy

The development of "inclusive language" materials for the regular worship of the church has raised significant theological issues: for example, the trinitarian nature of God, particularly the naming of the first and second persons of the triune God; the relationship between the eternal Christ and the historical, incarnate Jesus; the nature of sin; and the use of metaphor in theological language and liturgical prayer. These issues have been discussed throughout the process of the development and experimental use of new texts. But the proposed texts themselves have been the context for discussion, and often this conversation has occurred under the press of the triennial schedule of General Conventions and related publication deadlines. In 1993 the Standing Liturgical Commission sought to move away from the immediate urgency of creating new or revised supplemental liturgical materials, and address the theological and methodological issues posed by this endeavor.

The SLC worked to bring together scholars from various perspectives—liturgical studies, historical theology, systematic theology, biblical studies, and church history—with bishops, parish clergy, and laity. The resulting consultation, held at Seabury-Western Theological Seminary on September 9-11, 1993, included Episcopalian scholars from around the country, several of the Seabury-Western faculty, a few parish clergy and laity, and one bishop. The group prayed with the *Supplemental Liturgical Materials* throughout the three-day consultation and had several opportunities to reflect on their experience of prayer. The lay women from St. Luke's Episcopal Church, Evanston, Illinois, had worshipped with supplemental materials over a long period of time at their home parish, and they raised important concerns growing out of their experience with the texts.

The discussion of theological issues was built around three panel discussions. Each of the visiting scholars had prepared and circulated a position paper in advance of the consultation, and these papers were the basis for each discussion. Panelists responded to questions from a moderator and debated the issues among themselves, following which there was opportunity for both small and large group discussion. The materials in the following section include both the position papers and some of the dialogue from the consultation.

Participants in the Consultation

- The Rev. Dr. Paula S. Datsko Barker, Assistant Professor of Historical Theology, Seabury-Western Theological Seminary
- The Rev. Sr. Jean Campbell, Order of St. Helena, Vice Chair, Standing Liturgical Commission; member of the Consultation planning team; Chair of the Supplemental Liturgical Materials Committee
- Ms. Linda Cummings, Communicant, St. Luke's Episcopal Church, Evanston, Illinois
- Ms. Deborah DeManno, Communicant, St. Luke's Episcopal Church, Evanston, Illinois
- Dr. Robert Finster, Director of Music, Seabury-Western Theological Seminary
- The Rt. Rev. Frank T. Griswold, Bishop of Chicago; Chair, Standing Liturgical Commission

- Dr. Carolyn Groves, Senior Lecturer, Theology Department, Loyola University, Chicago; Communicant, St. Luke's Episcopal Church, Evanston, Illinois
- The Rev. Ralph N. McMichael, Jr., Instructor in Liturgics, Nashotah House Theological Seminary, Nashotah, Wisconsin
- The Rev. Dr. Ruth A. Meyers, Diocesan Liturgist, Diocese of Western Michigan; Associate Faculty member, Ecumenical Theological Center, Detroit, Michigan
- The Rev. Canon Leonel L. Mitchell, Professor of Liturgics, Seabury-Western Theological Seminary; member of the Standing Liturgical Commission; member of the Consultation planning team
- The Rev. Juan M. C. Oliver, doctoral student, Graduate Theological Union, Berkeley, California; Chair of the Standing Liturgical Commission Subcommittee on Inculturation of the Liturgy
- Ms. Lilian (Flower) Ross, Professor of Christian Ministry, Seabury-Western Theological Seminary
- The Rev. Joseph Russell, Canon to the Ordinary for Education and Program, Diocese of Ohio; member of the Standing Liturgical Commission; member of the Consultation planning team; member of the Supplemental Liturgical Materials Committee
- Mr. Newland F. Smith, Librarian and Associate Professor, Seabury-Western Theological Seminary
- The Rev. Dr. Taylor Stevenson, Professor of Philosophical Theology, Seabury-Western Theological Seminary
- The Rev. Dr. Patricia Wilson-Kastner, Rector, St. Ann and the Holy Trinity Episcopal Church, Brooklyn, New York
- The Rev. Dr. Charles Winters, Professor of Christian Ministry, Seabury-Western Theological Seminary
- Ms. Karla Woggan, Middler Student, Seabury-Western Theological Seminary; Chair, Supplemental Texts Task Force,

Seabury-Western Theological Seminary; Consultation Recorder

- The Rev. Dr. Ellen K. Wondra, Assistant Professor of Theological Studies, Colgate Rochester Divinity School/Bexley Hall/Crozer Theological Seminary, Rochester, New York

- The Rev. Dr. J. Robert Wright, Professor of Church History, The General Theological Seminary, New York, New York

Two members of the Consultation planning team were unable to attend the Consultation itself:

- The Rev. Dr. James Griffiss, Editor, Anglican Theological Review; (retired) Professor of Systematic and Philosophical Theology, Nashotah House Theological Seminary, Nashotah, Wisconsin

- The Rev. Joy Rogers, D.Min., Curate, St. Luke's Episcopal Church, Evanston, Illinois

Session One: Focus Questions

The Standing Liturgical Commission wants to explore the vast store of ancient liturgical prayer with a view of being able to bring forth images both new and old for the enrichment and enhancement of our present day liturgical life. In our search for new images and languages have we fully explored or honored the tradition of the church? How can we reclaim the ancient and often unfamiliar expressions of orthodox faithfulness that come out of the tradition of the church? Put another way, what does the tradition already offer that we may be overlooking?

What are appropriate ways in which biblical metaphors, images and descriptions of God can be put in the service of our liturgical prayer? In what ways is it appropriate to use diverse images of God in our liturgical prayer?

Translating the Tradition

J. Robert Wright

O f the four sets of questions that were posed in advance for this consultation, I have chosen to write upon the second: "How can we reclaim the ancient and often unfamiliar expressions of orthodox faithfulness that come out of the traditions of the church? Put another way, what does the tradition already offer that we may be overlooking?" Although the second set of questions was the only set that did not directly propose a discussion of God-language, I chose it because I have had some immediate experience in the human-language area. I suspected that many would focus upon language about God, as proposed in the other three sets of questions, but I offer this essay in the broader framework of the second set of questions and trust that it may at least enliven the consideration of other questions and possibly suggest some pointers for the way forward.

My recent major publication experience has been in editing and translating over four hundred fifty selections from Greek and Latin sources of the early church to serve as supplementary readings for the Daily Office of our Prayer Book calendar and liturgical year: *Readings for the Daily Office from the Early Church* (New York: Church Hymnal Corporation, 1991). Most of these already existed in English translations that were done decades or even centuries ago, but as I began to select them I soon realized that they were not adequate for our modern standards of linguistic inclusivity, and I could see that fresh translations were needed, at least for this purpose. I did not do very much with the God-language except to soften it, because I do not think the church as a whole wants much of that sort of change, at least not yet, and because the texts I was dealing with were actually not too bad on that score. The exclusive human-language was, in fact, much more jarring. But what I did do with the God-language was to soften it. Thus, for example, original sentences like: God is great, he is good, he is loving, he is kind, he is merciful, etc., I retranslated as: God is great, God is good, God is loving, etc. And original sentences like: the Father knows us, the Father sees us, the Father loves us, the Father protects us, etc., became: the Father knows us and sees us, loves us and protects us, etc. Thus, I softened the God-language, but I did not change the trinitarian persons. I am sure some of our other essays will be discussing this question, but my efforts were, and my remarks will now be, within the broader context that is delineated by the second set of questions: "What does the tradition already offer that we may be overlooking?"

In this light, the thesis as well as the conclusion of my paper will be to assert that the ancient common tradition of the first fifteen hundred Christian years offers us a great amount of valuable writing that can be recovered in a linguistically inclusive idiom precisely because it was written originally in Greek or Latin which, as regards human-language, are much more gender-neutral than is the case with our native English tongue. Another way to put my thesis, then, is to say that with the introduction of the English language tradition of the church, for which we as Anglicans bear a particular responsibility, there has regrettably been an increasing specificity and exclusivity of gender, both in original English composition and also in English translations of Greek and Latin sources. This has narrowed the scope of the original gender-free languages of Greek and Latin, and made the English renditions, and the resultant thought-patterns in those who use and pray our native tongue, a much more constricted and masculine-sounding universe of discourse than was ever the case in the original tongues that characterized the great period of the church before the rise of the English vernacular. And it is this highly gender-specific English vernacular that has so directly shaped our own more recent, and more narrow, Prayer Book tradition of the last four hundred fifty years. This is my thesis.

So what problems was I faced with, and how did I solve them? Most of the solutions I adopted can already be found in the principles of translators' license over the centuries, although they had been seldom used. Thus, Greek and Latin translated narrowly as "man" or "men" often became for me, depending upon the context, "one" or "they/them" or "we/us" or "humanity /humankind/ the human race." I often repeated a noun antecedent in substitution for a following pronoun that was gender-specific. And I used plural inclusive pronouns to refer to any antecedent noun in the collective singular; for example, in Bernard of Clairvaux's sermon on the feast of St. Andrew, I read close to the NRSV of Matthew 16:24: "If *any* wish to be my followers, let *them* deny *themselves* and take up *their* cross and follow me." And generally, in my retranslations for human beings, brethren became friends or beloved, craftsman became artist, steersman became pilot, seaman sailor, patrimony wealth or inheritance, freeman the free, schoolmaster schoolteacher, manhood adulthood or maturity, forefathers ancestors, madmen lunatics, and mortal men mere mortals.

Now some examples. In "The Word of God did not abandon men" of an earlier translation of Athanasius' *On the Incarnation*, the Greek τῶν ἀνθρώπων γένος became "the human race." Another: what was earlier translated as "How can a man hope for what he sees?" from Cyprian's *On the Value of Patience* 13:15, the Latin *Quod enim videt quis, quid sperat?* ultimately depending upon the Greek ὃ γὰρ βλέπει τίς ἐλπίζει of Romans 8:24, became "How can we hope for what is seen?" The famous passages in Irenaeus, *Against Heresies* 3-4, "God is man's glory" and "The glory of God is a living man, and the life of man is the vision of God" (*Gloria enim hominis Deus* and *Gloria enim Dei vivens homo, vita autem hominis visio Dei*) became "God is the glory of humanity" and "The glory of God is living humanity and the life of humanity is the vision of God." From Augustine's sermon 185, conventionally translated "He who glories, let him glory not in himself but in the Lord"

(*Qui gloriatur, non in se, sed in domino gloriatur*), I rendered "Let those who glory, glory not in themselves but in the Lord." And for Paul, an apostle "not from man, nor by any man," as found in Augustine's commentary on Galatians 1:1 (οὐκ ἀπ' ἀνθρώπων οὐδὲ δἰ ἀνθρώπου))\since it was Scripture that was being quoted, I settled with the NRSV's "sent neither by human commission nor from human authorities." Harder to call was my decision for Cyprian *On the Lord's Prayer*, where I read "to name ourselves children of God" (rather than "sons of God"), "even as Christ is *Son* of God," thus gaining human inclusivity for the first half of the phrase but surrendering the parallel between us as *sons* of God and Christ as *Son* of God. And Hilary of Poitiers *On the Trinity* quoting John 6:54-55, classically rendered in English as "He who eats my flesh and drinks my blood," I turned as "You who eat my flesh and drink my blood," even though the subject of the Greek text of John is third person singular. Such a shift from masculine third person singular to inclusive second person plural is not unknown in the history of English translating, but neither has it been very common in the past because the tendency of the English language in such cases, unlike the Greek, is toward exclusivity. The NRSV reads this "Those who...", which would have been another possibility.

Augustine's comment on I John 3:16, "As Christ laid down his life for us, so we too ought to lay down our lives for our brothers," his Latin reading *pro fratribus* and the New Testament Greek being ὑπὲρ τῶν ἀδελφῶν, became "for our sisters and brothers" in my translation, although I could have also accepted the NRSV "for one another." More difficult, though, was the same problem in a direct quotation from the Lord in Irenaeus, *Against Heresies* 4, "When you offer your gift at the altar and remember that your brother holds something against you," the Greek of Matthew 5:24 for brother reading ἀδελφός. To salvage this I opted for "your brother" followed by "[or sister]" in square brackets; the NRSV extends it to read "brother or sister" adding a footnote reading "Greek, *your brother*" in italics, but I decided this was not really a translation. I made another similar expansion for a homily of John

Chrysostom that also quoted words of the Lord: "As often as you did it for one of the least of my brothers [and sisters]." And I took a similar course for Hilary of Poitiers as he commented on Psalm 132, making it read "Behold how good and pleasant it is for brothers [and sisters] to dwell in unity," even though the NRSV here reads "when kindred live together in unity." This passage was made doubly difficult because Hilary continues "It is good for brothers (I added "[and sisters]") to dwell in unity, because when they do so their association creates their singleness of purpose." Perhaps, in retrospect, "kindred" would have been better here, but I felt that the imagery of "brothers dwelling in unity" was so deeply ingrained that it was better to extend it to include "sisters" than to substitute another word, thus retaining and expanding the familiar rather than opting for novelty. My final example of problems in human-language comes from Ignatius to the Ephesians speaking of "your bishop," where he says "you are as united with him as the church is to Jesus Christ." Here I left "him" as masculine because, even though my translations are intended primarily for use in a church that now ordains women to the episcopate, still the historical fact remains that the only bishops Ignatius could have been speaking of were men. This concludes my examples of the general principles I developed to achieve a more inclusive human-language.

The many instances of "Son of Man" formed a category all their own; in my book of 453 readings there were 21 of these. I decided to reject the usage of the Pueblo lectionary, "Man of Heaven" as being inaccurate and still exclusive; I did for a while consider the arguments for "Son of Humanity"; but in the end I voted with the NRSV to retain "Son of Man" unchanged. When it appears coupled with a human reference to "sons of God," though, I did still feel obliged to render the latter as "children of God" and this did result in surrendering several Latin theological parallels between *filius hominis* and *filii Dei*. Thus, as an example, for Leo the Great's sermon number 6 for Christmas, I read "the Savior, who became the Son of Man in order that we might have the power to be the children of God," even though the Latin sentence ended

Most difficult of all my translation problems was the category of references, and happily there were only a few of them, to Jesus as "man," historically accurate in the masculine gender, where the word "man" seemed to be making a theological point that would be lost now to our present North American religious consciousness if *homo* or ἄνθρωπος and occasionally even *vir* or ἀνήρ were not translated as inclusive and gender-free. These were hard cases to call, and I give some examples from the early church, a few of which are also combined with "Son of Man" phrases. For Irenaeus *Against Heresies* in the ICEL* text, the translation of a very difficult sentence that has held the field for the last ten or fifteen years in the English-speaking world of the Roman Catholic Church has read "The Word of God became man, the Son of God became the Son of Man, in order to unite man with himself and make him, by adoption, a son of God" (the Latin for "man" being *homo*). I rendered this more inclusively, "The Word of God became *human,* the Son of God became the Son of Man, in order to unite *us* with himself and make *us,* by adoption, *children and heirs* of God." Another example, where the word "man" seemed to be making a theological point that demands an inclusive translation even though it is making an historical reference to Jesus as male, was a phrase from Augustine's commentary on the Psalter, where the ICEL translation has hitherto held the field in English: "So that the Word might be both Son of God and Son of Man, one God with the Father and one man with all men" (*unus Deus cum Patre, unus homo cum hominibus*). This I translated less narrowly "One God with the Father and one *human being* with all *humankind.*" [I shall be interested to hear what alternative, if any, might be proposed for "Father" in a case like this.]

A few more examples of this "man" language and the solutions I adopted: Athanasius to Epictetus, "Our Savior truly became man,

*ICEL=International Commission on English in the Liturgy, a Roman Catholic body responsible for preparing English-language texts of Roman Catholic liturgical materials.

and from this has followed the salvation of men as a whole," I rendered anew in English as "Our Savior truly became *human*, and from this has followed the salvation of *humanity* as a whole." Augustine, sermon number 13 on the theme of the Nativity, where the English has conventionally but narrowly been rendered as "God became man so that men might become God; the Lord of the angels became man today so that men could eat the bread of angels," I put as follows: "God became *human like us* so that *we* might become God. The Lord of the angels became *one of us* today so that *we* could eat the bread of angels" (in each case my insertion of "human like us" and "one of us" enabled me to shift the result from an exclusive "men" to an inclusive "we"). I rendered Maximus the Confessor, "He is born as man," as "He is born as one of us." I reworked Cyril of Jerusalem, Catechesis 13, in this way: "It was not a mere man(ἄνθρωπος, for which I read "mere human being") who died for us, but the Son of God, God made man (ἐνανθρωπήσας, for which I read "God made human"). It was not a lowly man (ἄνθρωπος, for which I read "lowly human being") who suffered, but God incarnate." In Augustine's commentary on John, "If he is the head and we are the members, we form one complete man with him" (the Latin reading *totus homo, ille et nos*), I translated "one complete human being with him." And from the same passage, Augustine quoting Paul, "Till we become one in faith and in the knowledge of God's Son, and form that perfect man who is Christ come to full stature," I rendered Augustine's *virum perfectum* (which is the same in the Vulgate, the New Testament Greek being ἄνδρα τέλειον) as "perfect person." (The NRSV is even less direct or literal, and no more inclusive).

Continuing in the same, and most difficult, category of problem words, I faced Cyril of Alexandria commenting on John, "He is the bond that unites us, because he is at once both God and man"; for "man" I read "human." From a letter of Leo the Great, "He who in the nature of God had created man became in the nature of a servant man himself," I read "He who in the nature of God had created *humankind* became, in the nature of a servant, *human* himself." It is tempting to think of alternatives for "He" in both these last two examples, perhaps "Jesus" in the first case and "The One" in the second, but if that is done I think trinitarian presuppositions have to be clarified and also agreed upon. Finally, from the Easter homily of Melito of Sardis, "The lamb has become a Son, the Sheep a man, and man, God" (ὅ ἀμνὸς υἱός, καὶ τὸ πρόβατον ἄνθρωπος, καὶ ὅ ἄνθρωπος θεός), where the reference seems to be to the historical male Jesus but the doctrinal implications are clearly intended for all of us, I translated "The lamb has become a Son (no change), the sheep a *human*, and the *human* God."

These, therefore, illustrate the most difficult category I encountered in these translation problems: the references to Jesus as "man," historically accurate in the masculine gender, where however the word "man" seems to be making a theological point that would now be lost, at least to our present North American religious consciousness, if it were not translated as inclusive and gender-free. Many other references I also encountered, of course, to Jesus as *homo* or ἄνθρωπος, I took to be strictly historical references requiring the masculine translation as "man."

Now for some conclusions, as we have moved from general principles and examples of a more inclusive human-language in English translations to the unique case of "Son of Man" to the cases in which "man" is used with clear doctrinal implications:

1) The tradition of English language translation in theology is more narrow and constrictive than the Latin and Greek that preceded it, and we as Anglicans bear a special responsibility to rectify this.

2) Much of the first fifteen hundred years of Christian writing can be reclaimed in fresh translations that do no damage to their originals.

3) The entire subject before us is complex. The question of liturgical texts is only one part of the whole that cannot be solved in isolation by itself, and there are no easy answers.

4) Finally, I am convinced that proposals to expand or even alter the trinitarian language, which will no doubt be the subject of some of the other papers in this consultation, need to proceed even more carefully and systematically than the movement for retranslation to inclusive human-language, and I think they have an even greater obligation to seek clarification and agreement upon the presuppositions involved. When they talk about "Father" and "Son" in particular, whatever they say, they are using *English* words that were not part of the Christian vocabulary for nearly fifteen hundred years, and for this very reason I suggest that any proposal for change or alteration of such words will not be taken very seriously around the world and across the ecumenical spectrum unless it is proposed in terms of the wider tradition that preceded the constrictions of gender introduced by the English language. The implications of my own remarks for such proposals would necessitate still another paper that at present I have neither the space nor the time to write. And so instead, I end these remarks with some words of Gregory of Nyssa, commenting upon the Song of Songs:

"No one who has given thought to the way we talk about God can adequately grasp the terms pertaining to God. 'Mother,' for example, is mentioned [in the Song of Songs 3:11] instead of 'father.' Both terms mean the same, because there is neither male nor female in God. How, after all, could anything transitory like this be attributed to the Deity, when this is not permanent even for us human beings, since when we all become one in Christ we are divested of the signs of this difference along with the whole of our old humanity? Therefore every name we invent is of the same adequacy for indicating God's ineffable nature, since neither 'male' nor 'female' can defile the meaning of God's pure nature." [Migne, *Patrologiae Cursus Completus: Series Graeca* 44:916]

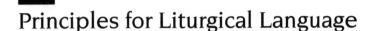

Principles for Liturgical Language

Ruth A. *Meyers*

"*What Language Shall I Borrow?*" asks the hymn writer Brian Wren as the title of a book.[1] Contemporary efforts to develop "inclusive language" liturgies have challenged Christians of many denominations to find appropriate ways to speak of God and to God in worship. It is no small task, for, as Gail Ramshaw has pointed out, to recast liturgical language "one must know the gospel, the tradition, and the contemporary situation, and must hold them together in liturgical language."[2]

The Language of the People

Worship in the language of the people is an important liturgical principle. The sixteenth-century Reformers called for worship in the vernacular. The first (1789) Prayer Book of the Episcopal Church updated archaic language, for example, replacing "which" with "who." Numerous linguistic changes were made in the 1979 Prayer Book to provide worship in contemporary language. Changing formal address from "thou" to "you" and updating third person singular verb endings are obvious changes. Less apparent are such things as altering word order, shortening sentences, and occasionally inverting the order of ideas.[3] Deliberate effort was also made to eliminate generic uses of masculine nouns and pronouns. Little or nothing was done with respect to God-language, although the "Committee on Sensitivity Relating to Women" recommended not only rewording language about humanity but also de-emphasizing masculine God-language.

It is not sufficient, however, simply to call for worship "in the language of the people." The language of everyday discourse is often not suitable for liturgical prayer. Worship is a more significant occasion than everyday encounters, and the language used should reflect that. The language of a formal political speech or a commencement address, for example, differs from that of ordinary conversation. Likewise, the language of worship should be more eloquent and carefully considered than casual conversation.

While liturgical language should be stately and eloquent, it is not an exercise in articulating doctrine. Doctrinal considerations may influence liturgical revision, as, for example, in the 1928 Prayer Book in the inclusion of prayers for the departed and the elimination of a prayer which suggested that disastrous weather was a divine retribution for sin. But worship is not a didactic inculcation of orthodox theology. Rather, worship is itself primary theology: the people of God encountering God through Word and Sacrament. The language of worship establishes and facilitates that encounter.

In search of appropriate liturgical language, the suggestion is sometimes made to turn to poetry. But poetic language is not necessarily suitable. Gail Ramshaw points out that poetry does not require an external point of reference, for example, the original audience. Poetry has meaning in and of itself, through its own aesthetic effect.[4] In contrast, liturgical language has meaning in the context of the worshiping community. Liturgy is a corporate enterprise: the people of God gathered to offer praise and thanks to God, to recall God's wondrous deeds, to be formed anew as God's people in the world. The language of worship must be such that it can be shared by the people gathered.

To describe the nature of liturgical language, many contemporary writers have turned to the category of metaphor. Much of our language about God, both within and beyond the liturgy, must be metaphorical in order to speak of the ineffable and inexhaustible mystery of God.

The Use of Metaphor

In metaphor, two thoughts or concepts are held together in tension or interaction with each other. Metaphor is not a simple comparison. Rather, the two elements of the metaphor are both similar and dissimilar. Metaphor takes two images that appear disparate, puts them together, and invites comparisons and associations. "Metaphors can organize thinking, encourage a transfer of associations and feelings between the matrices they intersect, extend language, generate new insights, and move us at a deep level by their appeal to the senses and imagination."[5]

While much language about God is metaphorical, commentators disagree as to how much is metaphor. G.B. Caird claims, "All, or almost all, of the language used by the Bible to refer to God is metaphor (the one possible exception is the word 'holy')."[6] Sandra Schneiders identifies at least four types of language about God in the Old Testament: literal designations (e.g., God as liberator, God as covenant-maker); names for God (the tetragrammaton); personifications of God (Wisdom and Shekinah, the rabbinic term for the biblical experience of God's presence in, for example, the pillar of cloud); and metaphors.[7]

Father as a Metaphor for God

Particularly crucial is the question of whether "Father" is a metaphor. Alvin Kimel argues vehemently that Father is "a name and filial term of address *revealed* by God himself in the person of his Son."[8] The origins of this assertion can be traced to the research of Joachim Jeremias, who claimed that "*abba*" was an unprecedented title used by Jesus to express his unique and intimate relationship with God.[9] But Jeremias' conclusions have been called into question by a number of scholars.

While Jeremias argued that *abba* was an intimate form of address akin to "Daddy," others find little textual and philological support for this position. James Barr concludes that although *abba* was used colloquially in Jesus' time, it was not a childish expression, but "more a solemn, responsible, adult address to a father."[10]

Jeremias also claimed that *abba* was an unprecedented personal address to God, not found in the practice of ancient Judaism and thus unique to Jesus. But this conclusion has been contested by Jewish scholars.[11] More recently Eileen Schuller has published a Hebrew text from Qumran, dating from about the first century B.C.E., that includes a prayer in which Joseph addresses God as "my father and my God." Schuller refers to another prayer text from Qumran that seems to close with the address "my father and my lord."[12] Taken with other Hebrew and Greek texts rejected by Jeremias on various grounds, they provide substantial evidence to challenge Jeremias' claim that Jesus' address of God as "father" was distinct from the use of ancient Judaism.[13]

Most significant are those studies which challenge the assertion that the use of *abba* is central to Jesus' understanding of God or to Jesus' prayer. Jeremias concluded that all addresses to the Father by Jesus in the Gospels derive from an original *abba*. Barr counters that the wide variation in the Greek forms of "father" used in the Gospels reflects not different translations of the single word *abba*, but "different expressions of the generally received tradition that Jesus addressed God as Father." According to Barr, the different uses of "father" may translate different Semitic terms or may have originated in the Greek tradition and thus have no precise Semitic original. In a review of the pertinent synoptic texts, Madeleine Boucher posits that at most four texts might be authentic sayings of Jesus, of which only one is an address in prayer: the Lord's Prayer. Boucher and Barr both conclude that the available evidence makes it difficult to prove the centrality of the use of *abba* by Jesus and thus calls into question the view that "father" is central to Jesus' understanding of God.[14]

More recently Mary Rose D'Angelo has considered the use of "father" in the literary, social, and political contexts of ancient Judaism and Christianity. She concludes that the use of "father" cannot be said to have originated with Jesus or to be particularly important to his teaching. If "father" was used by Jesus, it is likely that it did not reflect a unique or special intimacy of Jesus with

God, but rather may have been used to call into question Caesar's reign and to make a claim upon God's protection, mercy, and providence. D'Angelo asserts that this latter use of "father" was particularly important in Jewish literature.[15]

A different explanation of Jesus' understanding of God is presented by Raymond Brown. Reviewing the use of the "I am" formula in John, Brown proposes that the divine name given to Jesus and revealed by Jesus to the disciples is "I AM." Brown considers whether the phrase "I am" is a Johannine creation, and on the basis of four synoptic passages (Mark 14:62, cf. Luke 22:70; Matt. 14:27; Luke 24:36; Mark 13:6, cf. Luke 21:8) he suggests that the Johannine use may elaborate on the use of "I am" already attributed to Jesus in the synoptic tradition.[16]

Brown's thesis and the challenges to Jeremias' work dispute the claim that Father is *the* name for God revealed by Jesus. Brian Wren contests the distinction between a revealed name and a metaphor. Wren argues that divine revelation cannot be distinguished from metaphors arising from human experience: "if God reveals Godself to us, it has to be in language drawn from the particularities of our physical makeup and our political, economic, and cultural experience." Thus the term Father is drawn from human experience, just as other metaphors for God (e.g., "rock" [Psalm 95:1], "she-bear" [Hosea 13:8], "potter" [Jer. 18:1-11]) reflect human experience. As metaphors, these terms and other scriptural metaphors intersect with "God" and so provide ways to conceive of God. They are not to be understood as identical with God, but rather, as metaphors, are both like and unlike God. "Father" may express God's care for us and authority over us, but God is not literally a male human being who has sexual intercourse with a female and so engenders a child.[17]

While *abba* may not be central to Jesus' self-understanding, there is little doubt that Father is an important metaphor in the Christian tradition. But it must be placed alongside other metaphors for God. Sandra Schneiders, who takes a less critical view of Jeremias' work, points to Jesus' use of feminine images and metaphors for God and concludes that Jesus understood God in feminine as well as masculine terms. Hence "the male metaphors are not to be literalized or absolutized."[18]

Alvin Kimel acknowledges the existence of feminine imagery for God in the scriptures, but claims that feminine terms are always used in the form of simile and not metaphor and so "cannot be given equal status with the foundational masculine imagery" of the Bible. According to Kimel, in a simile two things are compared in a specific and self-limiting way, while in metaphor the two elements are placed together in a manner that invites further insight and imaginative thinking.[19] Without disputing the distinction between simile and metaphor, it is difficult to see how a feminine image such as "the rock that bore you...the God who gave you birth" (Deut. 32:18) functions as simile and not as metaphor.

The feminine images of God, while far less extensive than masculine images, should be given particular consideration in light of the patriarchal culture in which the scriptures were written. That feminine metaphors appear in spite of this cultural bias suggest that they convey important truth about God: that God cannot be understood in exclusively masculine terms, that God is neither male nor female. Schneiders asserts that even the masculine images do not legitimize the reigning patriarchal culture. For example, in Hosea, God, a husband whose wife has played the harlot, does not behave as a patriarch and divorce the unfaithful wife, but remains faithful and seeks reconciliation. In the parable of the prodigal son, the father refuses to assert patriarchal superiority and privilege and instead offers loving forgiveness. According to Schneiders, Jesus' presentation of the father subverts human structures of patriarchy by invalidating an appeal to divine institution.[20]

Naming the Triune God

I have argued that Father should be viewed as a metaphor rather than the revealed name of God; that this metaphor must be viewed in the context of other metaphors, particularly feminine metaphors, for God; and that the masculine metaphors often subvert rather than uphold human patriarchy. While these factors could be taken to support the reduction of Father-language in liturgical prayer, the question of trinitarian theology must be addressed. The naming of the triune God as Father, Son, and Holy Spirit has occupied a central place in Christian tradition and cannot be lightly dismissed.

In popular thought, the Trinity is often viewed as an esoteric mystery, a mystery which points to the inner workings of the divine but has little connection to daily life. Even the term "the Trinity" suggests a static entity remote from us. The dominant approach of Western theology for many centuries has been to formulate theories about the immanent Trinity, the relationship of Father, Son, and Spirit to each other independent of their relationship to humanity.[21]

A different approach to trinitarian theology begins with the economic Trinity, God for us. From this perspective, what is significant about the triune God is that God's very nature is to be in relationship, both within God's self and with us. In Jesus' use of *abba*, *abba* is not an ontological statement about the essence of God, but rather an expression of how God relates to Jesus. The salient point is the relationship, not the masculine terms Father and Son. Catherine LaCugna proposes that other analogies, some already found in antiquity, could also express effectively this self-relatedness of God: Mother-Daughter, Father-Daughter, Mother-Son, Lover-Beloved, Friend-Friend.[22]

Not only is God self-related, God by God's very nature relates to us. We know this relational God through the events of salvation history, in particular through the events of creation, incarnation, and the sending of the Spirit. This has led to the increasingly common naming of God as "Creator, Redeemer, and Sanctifier (or Sustainer)." But to name God by identifying God's functions in the economy of salvation is in itself inadequate. It suggests that there are three persons, each responsible for a different function, and does not convey the truth that the triune God creates, the triune God redeems, the triune God sanctifies and sustains. Furthermore, as LaCugna points out, functional or modalist language "does not sufficiently highlight the personal and relational character of God *as God.* The strong and bold claim of trinitarian theology is that not only is God related to us, but it is the very *essence* or *substance* of God to be relational."[23]

What seems to be needed is more than a different way to name the Trinity, whether those names are functional or relational. New names are important, but they must be accompanied by a shift in thinking, a shift from a static ontological view of the Trinity to a dynamic relational understanding of the triune God. LaCugna suggests that Christian worship is trinitarian not primarily because it names God as Father, Son, and Spirit, but because worship celebrates the mystery of God's redemptive love for us.[24]

Naming God in Worship

To speak of God and to God in worship, we need a variety of forms, not just names for God. The collect form may be an especially useful resource. The classical form of a collect begins with an invocation or address to God and frequently includes an attribution stating the basis for the petition that follows. For example, the Morning Prayer Collect for Fridays begins, "Almighty God, whose most dear Son went not up to joy but first he suffered pain." The use of a variety of descriptive adjectives and clauses may be one way in which to expand the language and imagery used for God. In *A New Zealand Prayer Book,* a collect for Good Friday begins, "Crucified savior, naked God"; a collect for the twenty-second Sunday after Pentecost addresses "God, the mother and father of us all."[25]

The use of descriptive adjectives and clauses need not be limited to collects. *Intercessions for the Christian People,* although primarily using variations of "Lord, have mercy," and "Lord, hear our prayer," includes also a few corporate responses such as, "O God of wonder, hear our prayer," and "O God, holding the world with love, have mercy on us."[26] The opening acclamations for the Eucharist and opening versicles and salutation at the prayers in the Daily Offices can also make use of a variety of images for God.

More extended prayers, the eucharistic prayer and, to a lesser extent, the confession of sin and the postcommunion prayer, can make use of an even wider range of metaphors. Sallie McFague, describing metaphorical theology, asserts that "a piling up of images is essential, both to avoid idolatry and to attempt to express the richness and variety of the divine-human relationship."[27] The same can be said of liturgical prayer. This is not so much "inclusive" language as it is "expansive" language, the use of multiple metaphors to speak of the inexhaustible mystery of God.

The most obvious source for expansive language is scripture. But this does not tell us which metaphors will work in liturgical prayer. Some scriptural metaphors included in Prayer Book Studies 30 met significant resistance: "reach out your saving arm," "cords of compassion and bands of love," "as a hen gathers her young." One problem seemed to be that people were ignorant of scripture, and this will be a continuing problem in this contemporary world where so many Christians are biblically illiterate. Further difficulty is posed by the multiplicity of translations of the Bible, so that a reference to scripture may not be recognized due to unfamiliarity with the particular translation used.[28]

Even when the scriptural referent is recognized, the metaphor may arouse objection. McFague lists stages of metaphor identified by Colin Turbayne. In the first stage, a newly coined metaphor seems inappropriate or unconventional and may be rejected. At a second stage, a living metaphor has both literal and metaphorical meaning and is insightful.[29] The challenge to liturgical revisers is to present new metaphors that can overcome the initial shock and become living metaphor that stimulates imaginative thinking in the church. Experimental use of texts may be the best way both to provide sufficient familiarity to allow new metaphors to move to the second stage and to weed out metaphors that are widely rejected. In this way, new metaphors can become the prayer of the people.

Conclusion

The development of inclusive-language or expansive-language liturgies has been a response to feminist concerns about masculine God-language. But we should not limit ourselves to the question of what language should or should not be used to speak of God and to God. What is needed is a renewed understanding of the tri-une God, whose very essence is relational, who pours Godself forth upon us, and who invites us to share in the riches of divine life. New and revised liturgical forms should draw upon a wide range of biblical metaphor so that our worship may continue to celebrate the wonder and mystery of the triune God and might inspire our imaginations and so draw us deeper into the mystery of God.

Notes

1. Brian Wren, *What Language Shall I Borrow?* (New York: Crossroad, 1990).

2. Gail Ramshaw-Schmidt, *Christ in Sacred Speech* (Philadelphia: Fortress, 1986), p. 4.

3. Charles P. Price, *Introducing the Draft Proposed Book*, Prayer Book Studies 29 (New York: Church Hymnal, 1976), pp. 24-6.

4. Ramshaw-Schmidt, p. 3.

5. Wren, p. 92.

6. *The Language and Imagery of the Bible* (Philadelphia: Westminster, 1980), p. 18.

7. Sandra Schneiders, *Women and the Word* (New York and Mahwah: Paulist, 1986), pp. 20-28.

8. "A New Language for God?" (Shaker Heights, Ohio: Episcopalians United, 1990), p. 11; emphasis in original.

9. *The Prayers of Jesus*, trans. John Bowden, Studies in Biblical

10. "Abba Isn't Daddy," *Journal of Theological Studies* 39 (1988):46. See also Geza Vermes, *Jesus and the World of Judaism* (London, 1983), pp. 41-3; Joseph Fitzmyer, *A Wandering Aramaean* (Missoula, Montana: Scholars, 1979), pp. 134-5, cited by Mary Collins, "Naming God in Public Prayer," *Worship* 59 (1985):296.

11. Mary Rose D'Angelo, "*Abba* and 'Father': Imperial Theology and the Jesus Traditions," *Journal of Biblical Literature* 111 (1992):613, cites several scholars who dispute Jeremias' claim.

12. Eileen Schuller, "4Q372 1: A Text about Joseph," *Revue de Qumran* 14 (1990):343-70; Schuller, "The Psalm of 4Q372 1 within the Context of Second Temple Prayer," *Catholic Biblical Quarterly* 54 (1992):67-79; cited by D'Angelo, p. 618.

13. Jeremias rejected Hebrew and Aramaic texts that use "father" in prayer but not as a direct address; Jewish texts in Greek because he did not see those as possible influences on Jesus; and evidence from biblical and Jewish sources that reflected a "corporate" rather than "personal" understanding of God as father. D'Angelo has argued that there are significant continuities in the use of father in these various ancient Hebrew and Greek texts: D'Angelo, "Theology in Mark and Q: *Abba* and 'Father' in Context," *Harvard Theological Review* 85 (1992):152; see also "*Abba* and 'Father'," pp. 619-22.

14. Barr, pp. 41-7, quotation on p. 44; Madeleine Boucher, "The Image of God in the Gospels: Towards a Reassessment" (address to the Catholic Biblical Association, Aug. 1984), cited by Collins, pp. 296-7.

15. D'Angelo, "*Abba* and 'Father'," pp. 621, 630; "Theology in Mark and Q," pp. 161-62, 172-74.

16. *The Gospel According to John (i-xii)*, Anchor Bible, Vol. 29 (Garden City, N.Y.: Doubleday, 1966), pp. 533-8; see Collins, pp. 297-98.

17. Wren, pp. 95-102; see also Schneiders, pp. 25-6.

18. Schneiders, pp. 37-41, quotation on p. 41.

19. Kimel, "A New Language for God?", pp. 4-5. Wren, p. 86, makes a similar distinction between simile and metaphor.

20. Schneiders, pp. 32-34, 45-49.

21. Catherine Mowry LaCugna, "Making the Most of Trinity Sunday," *Worship* 60 (1986):212-3.

22. "The Baptismal Formula, Feminist Objections, and Trinitarian Theology," *Journal of Ecumenical Studies* 26 (1989):241-6. LaCugna is not speaking specifically of liturgical language when she proposes these analogies.

23. Ibid., pp. 243-4, emphasis in original; see also LaCugna, "Problems with a Trinitarian Reformulation," *Louvain Studies* 10 (1985):330.

24. "Making the Most of Trinity Sunday," pp. 210-2.

25. [Anglican] Church of the Province of New Zealand, *A New Zealand Prayer Book* (London: Collins, 1989), pp. 588, 633.

26. Gail Ramshaw, ed., *Intercessions for the Christian People: Prayers of the People for Cycles A, B, and C of the Roman, Episcopal, and Lutheran Lectionaries* (Collegeville, Minn.: Pueblo, 1988), pp. 106-7.

27. Sallie McFague, *Metaphorical Theology* (Philadelphia: Fortress, 1982), p. 20.

28. Paul F. Bradshaw, "The Use of the Bible in Liturgy," *Studia Liturgica* 22 (1992):44; see also Thomas H. Troeger, *Imagining a Sermon* (Nashville: Abingdon, 1990), pp. 41-3.

29. Colin M. Turbayne, *The Myth of Metaphor* (New Haven, Conn.: Yale, 1962), pp. 24-5, cited by McFague, p. 41.

Session One: Panel Discussion

Paula Barker, Ruth Meyers, Leonel Mitchell, Robert Wright

Excerpts from the panel discussion

What does the tradition offer that we may be overlooking? How do we embolden the tradition? Dare we look beyond our own tradition?

Liturgical prayer is the prayer of the church and therefore the people of God must be able to find themselves in that prayer and enter into the mystery of God. The beginning point must be scripture. If we can identify our language as having resonance with the Gospel then it is worth trying to work with it.

The Bible question is certainly important as a place to begin, but we need to realize that some of the great doctrines of the church are not clearly set forth in the Bible and yet the doctrines have been accepted in the church for generations.

It is possible to find things in scripture and in patristic theology, but it will not pray well because the categories are too foreign to the congregation. Actually, one of our problems with the liturgical texts we already have is that what people hear and understand is often not what is intended by the text. Our job is not to invent a new religion but to find images and words that allow the authentic images of the text to come through without overtones that resonate in negative ways.

I assumed twenty years ago that all devotional material used masculine language especially since art and architecture that I was familiar with used only male images. But then I began to realize that in medieval times and in the Romanesque period there was a strong devotion to divine Wisdom that was personified as a woman. This female figure of Wisdom was pictured as the throne of the Christ child. "In the lap of the mother dwells the wisdom of the Father." Perhaps we need to look to medieval art as a place to find more expansive images of God. We certainly need to look to paintings and sculpture as well as written sources.

Devotional texts coming out of the same period spoke of the second person as Wisdom—a female persona. We read of Christ on the cross birthing forth new creation and our souls as the church of God. Christ on the cross is understood as the mother in labor birthing a new creation. A medieval writer talked of Christ on the bed of the cross with veins ruptured as Christ gives birth to the new creation. In another image we read of Christ as a nursing mother. The wound in Christ's side is an outflow of divine Wisdom. Bernard of Clairvaux wrote of Jesus as a nursing mother, and he would advise those in spiritual struggle to "suck not the wounds but the breast of the Christ crucified." Then he went on to apply that kind of imagery to himself. He felt for his monks as a mother felt for her children. When he left his monks he was as a mother leaving the child torn from her breast.

What is the good news that our communities need to hear? Julian perceived in her time a predominant sense of God as an awful majestic God who inspired debilitating fear that led to despair and a giving up of the faith. She developed language of the motherhood of God because it would offer hope to the community instead of despair. Calvin used the image of Father to accomplish the same thing.

In retranslating we need to be aware of how exclusivity has crept into the English-language tradition. There has been a narrowing of tradition with translation from ancient language. "He" and "him" repeated time and time again in English texts are not present in the original text. There is opportunity to do much more by retranslating Greek rather than trying to revise sixteenth-century texts that are heavily masculine.

Not everything from tradition or scripture will work as the prayer of the church. That is why we need not only to look to the tradition, but try out the prayers in worshiping communities as well. We can't just lift phrases from tradition or scripture.

There is need for a longer period of time to live with this process of hearing new language. We must deal with the language issue in the same painstaking way we dealt with women's ordination a generation ago. The things we are talking about here, such as the seat of Wisdom, must become more of a common part of the language in the Anglican church. These things need to be spread out and experienced over a longer period of time.

Response from the participants

The voice of the child is important. Using "men and women" still leaves out the child. Language must expand the imagination. The piling-on of many images may help to take us to the edge where we find God. This is what the prayer language of the early church did. Look at the rich and varied imagery of Eucharistic Prayer D, for example. Liturgical prayer tended to get fixed and constricted over time.

We need to go to the marginalized and hear what they are dreaming. How do they image God? Prayers must be accessible for everyone, but how do you maintain the balance?

A strategy for further experimentation and dialogue would be to write collects that would introduce new metaphors and images. The present collects include a wide range of imagery, but they tend to use very masculine terms. Collects would be a good place to go in terms of future work. Ironically, the medieval collects were more expansive in imagery than the more contemporary collects. As we talk about the collects, however, we need to ask if the rhetorical structure of the Prayer Book collects is worth saving. Why should Americans pray in a way that is so alien to the culture? We need to ask what American rhetoric sounds like. How do we speak with solemnity in our public places? Write collects in that vein rather than in the traditional structure.

Ideally, the people of the community have a hand in fashioning the prayer, otherwise they cannot enter into that prayer. How do we get people into the process of owning the prayer? We are assuming that as a community we can voice the prayer of the church when in fact the community does not have a voice.

For many of our people, Sunday morning is the only time for prayer, and thus what we pray, sing and say carries a lot of weight. People don't want to deal with a community that will challenge them. They come to be comforted; thus there can be a tension between the individual's need and the community's need.

The development of metaphors is crucial. Is it possible to speak of an analogical relationship of metaphors? Would that open them up without losing continuity? Julian took the kingly image of God and emphasized the servant aspect of Christ. Out of her reflection on "Lord" and "servant," the motherhood image emerged for her. How are the images related; and when similar and dissimilar images are played off against the other, how does it affect our understanding of God?

Session Two: Focus Questions

How do we name the Trinity? Specifically, how do we name the first and second persons of the Trinity?

Gender and Trinitarian Language

Ellen K. *Wondra*

In this paper I will discuss some ways in which the perennial problem of how we address the Trinity is complicated by our failure to examine assumptions about gender. I write as a professing Christian, a woman, a priest, and a teaching theologian. I also write out of twenty years' experience with inclusive-language worship in widely varied congregations in many parts of the country.

Over the last several months, I have concluded, reluctantly and sadly, that the accustomed formula for the Trinity, "Father, Son, and Holy Spirit," will remain the primary (but not exclusive) one, at least for the time being. This is not because we have concluded that there is some eternal merit or status attached to this formula as the normative one. We have not yet looked at the full meaning of this imagery because we have been unwilling to look at the relation of figurative speech to the contexts in which it arises and is used. Also, we have only recently begun to develop adequate liturgical forms that will allow us to glimpse the divine reality in ways other than customary ones. Indeed, until we do these things, I don't think we have yet established the conditions that can warrant a normative conclusion about any form of naming God. The rest of this paper will give some idea of what I mean by these statements.

Let me begin with two deliberately provocative questions.

Question 1:

Why not call the Second Person of the Trinity "God the Daughter"?

Calling the Second Person of the Trinity "God the Daughter" is unlikely, I suspect, because Jesus was a man. The Second Person, eternally begotten by the First, became human in male form; therefore, it is "natural" to call the Second Person "Son." But this masks at least two important elements in our understanding of the Trinity and the Incarnation.

In relation to salvation, the maleness of Jesus has no ultimate meaning. As the church Fathers recognized, "What was not assumed is not redeemed." This means that unless it is the humanity of Jesus which matters, rather than his maleness, women are not redeemed. The fact that Jesus was a male human being, coupled with the Christian tradition's long-standing androcentric preference for masculine images for God, has produced ages of confusion about the importance of Jesus' gender, with consequent distortions of church discipline as well as doctrine. In some branches of Christianity, these confusions and distortions continue today.

Second: According to the classical doctrine of the Trinity, the name of each Person of the Trinity first and foremost reflects the relation of that Person to the others, and then derivatively to any element of creation. That is, the "names" of the Persons give their relation to each other, rather than to some characteristic which is possessed in itself. One way of expressing the relation between the First and Second Persons is a begotten and unbegotten begetter. Or—to put it in ostensibly more personal terms—the Father is the Father because the Father is the Father of the Son. Without the Son, the Father is not, indeed cannot be, the Father, even as the Son cannot be the Son without the Father. There are other relational terms, such as Logos/Word and Sophia/Wisdom for the Second Person, or the plurality of terms (e.g., lover and beloved related through love) found in Augustine's great treatise *De Trinitate*. All of these, like Son or Daughter, convey the belief that the Second Person of the Trinity is an authentic expression and continuation of the First Person without being identical to the First Person. Within the context of creation, the Second Person gives full and authentic expression and embodiment to the First.

In sum: The precise historical particularities—gender, race, class, nationality—in which God became incarnate do not change the fundamental relationship between the First and Second Persons of the Trinity. And it is this fundamental relationship, rather than what each Person is like alone, that is crucial. The attribution of one gender rather than the other to the Second Person is connected with the historic and human reality of the Incarnation, but it has no salvific relevance.

Question 2:

Why not call the First Person of the Trinity "God the Mother"?

Answering this is a little more complicated. The negative answers given in the current discussion can be summarized as follows. The First Person cannot be called "Mother" because:

1. Jesus' preferred manner for addressing God is "Father," and in the Lord's Prayer he taught us to do the same. Christianity has been and should be faithful to this.

2. The First Person of the Trinity begets the Second; that is, the Second is not an emanation from the First.

3. It is not appropriate to call God "Mother" because this name conveys too close an identification between God and nature/creation (as in the Goddess-worshiping fertility religions). This identification compromises God's freedom and therefore God's sovereignty.

4. "Father" is God's "personal" name and so has a status different from all other names. When used of God, the term "Father" is not gendered. "Mother," however, is a gendered term.

Therefore, for one or more of these reasons, the formula "Father, Son, and Holy Spirit" is subject to neither substitution nor replacement.

What is to be made of these responses?

First: It is not at all clear that Jesus himself used the term "Father" either as exclusively or as normatively as is claimed. Nor is it clear that the normative status of naming the Trinity as Father,

Son, and Holy Spirit is either as ancient or as universal as is claimed; there are other biblical and liturgical candidates as well, even if this is the one most familiar to us. In other words, the claim that the name "Father" is normative even in scripture and tradition is not as compelling as it may at first appear.

The other three answers are of a theological rather than historical-biblical nature. I want to draw attention to the hidden assumptions concerning gender in these answers. Point four claims that the term "Father" is not gendered when applied to God because God is beyond body, parts, and passions. Yet the same is not felt to be true of the term "Mother." Why not? I suspect the reason here is similar to the reason that "man" may be taken as universal whereas "woman" may not: in "common sense usage" until recently that which is associated with femaleness always has a gender, whereas that which is associated with maleness does not. The male presents and represents what is universal as well as maleness, ostensibly transcending gender and any other particular human characteristic (such as race or nationality). This is one very important element of the androcentrism of Western thought, culture, and religion: the male is the normative human being, and the female is a subclass of or deviation from the norm.

However, the matter of gender is more complicated than simply the use of obviously gendered terms like father, mother, son, daughter, he, or she. Gender also has to do with character attributes and personality traits. Let us look more closely at answers two and three to the second question. Both suggest that motherliness— femaleness—inherently has to do with close relation, identification, and compromise of freedom in a way that fatherliness— maleness—does not. This view is related to the patriarchal association of maleness with freedom and femaleness with dependence and contingency. Moreover, according to answer two, fathers beget beings who are thereafter separate from themselves, while mothers give birth to beings from within themselves (mothers do not beget, they give birth). The suggestion is, further, that the close relation represented by the female may (does?) readily become inordinate. Imaging God in female-gendered terms is then problematic when one of the primary attributes of God is freedom (in the sense of non-dependence and non-necessity).

The reference to fertility cults also suggests that the problem here is the close identification of femaleness with the body, with sexuality, with reality that has not been shaped (the natural), and with contingency. Complementing this is the close identification of maleness with the spirit, with mind and will, with reality that has been shaped (the historical), and with freedom or autonomy. It is significant that the qualities associated with maleness are also attributes of God, who is, in fact, traditionally seen as the exemplar and source of these attributes. Indeed, enormous theological energy has been devoted over the centuries to demonstrating precisely how God can be related to the material world without in any sense compromising "His" freedom, autonomy, non-necessity, sovereignty, and creativity. Meanwhile, the complementary qualities are associated with creatureliness and sometimes with sin; i.e., they are associated with what is not-God.

Now, I have said that all this has to do with gender. Gender, as compared to sex, is a construct of human culture and history, reflecting and reinforcing social arrangements that incorporate biological differences of sex and give them their social importance. The difference between gender and sex is evident in part because different societies often have very different gender arrangements. This indicates that what we see as "naturally" male or female is in fact socially constructed; it is, therefore, also subject to change. Indeed, our current constructions of gender are relatively recent and significantly incorporate constructions of race and class as well. And yet, because we most readily see gender as a given, we do not see the assumptions about gender that may be embedded in discussions of seemingly unconnected matters.

It should also be noted that gender is a terribly important category in human life. The first question we have about a newborn concerns its sex; as soon as that question is answered, our behavior toward and expectations of that baby take shape. Indeed, we cannot imagine what a "person" is without some attribution of gender. The level of interest directed toward the ungendered character Pat on *Saturday Night Live* and toward the "central secret" of the film *The Crying Game* are contemporary indications of this. But it is indicated also in the claim that certain terms for God—Word, Wisdom, Creator, Parent, Child, Only-Begotten, and others—are impersonal and therefore not really adequate for address of a personal God. These terms are anthropomorphic, but they are not obviously gendered. And that, I suggest, is why they are felt to be impersonal. Gender, then, has "person-making" significance in our culture. If that is correct, the question facing us is not *whether* we will imagine a personal God in gender-laden terms; rather, it is *how* we will do so.

I think a crucial aspect of answering that question is further consideration of what we mean by "person." I have already suggested that gender is a "person-making" characteristic in the formal sense that we cannot easily imagine a person without a gender. It is also person-making substantively, in that we in Western cultures have tended to view true persons as those possessed of freedom, self-determination (in some degree), individuality, and autonomy—qualities associated with maleness.

However, there is another substantive component of becoming a person, and that is relationality. This component has been brought to the fore recently, particularly by feminist theorists, but it is in fact an ancient concept. Persons do not exist apart from their relationships. This is literally true in that each one of us is born out of a relationship. But it is also true in the more figurative sense that we do not know who or how we are except in and through those and that to which we are related.

Our customary language for the Trinity is exemplary of exactly this concept, once we allow ourselves to ask why the Persons of the Trinity are named as they are. The "names" of the Persons of the

Trinity first and foremost reflect the relation of each Person to the others. Two of the Persons are named in the gendered kinship terms "Father" and "Son" precisely because the First Person is related to the Second as one who begets yet is unbegotten, while the Second is begotten. Unless these two relationships pertained, we could not name these Persons in this way. But note that there are two elements to these familiar terms: kinship, where neither one has identity without the other; and gender.

Gender itself is a relational construct. One's gender is known only in relation to a range of possibilities. Each of us understands the character and meaning of our own maleness and femaleness only in relation to the maleness and femaleness of others. But given the prevailing androcentric undertow of our culture, we tend to see gender as a "given," i.e., as not relational. And that, I have suggested, is in part because culturally we put higher value on and attribute universality to the qualities traditionally associated with maleness, especially the qualities of autonomy and freedom from necessity.

But this does not mean that other terms are not also relational. That is, the Holy Spirit is so named because the Holy Spirit is the Spirit *of*—that is, in a particular relation to—the other two Persons. The Holy Spirit has no existence in and of itself. The same is true of the other two Persons as well. The Word is always the Word *of* somebody, for example. Careful reflection will show that this is true of other names as well, though we are less accustomed to thinking of them in this way.

In some ways that is my first point: we are not *accustomed* to thinking in this way. This very preliminary exploration of relationality indicates its importance. It also indicates that gender is only one way of describing relationship. But this fact has been hidden, and its very hiddenness contributes to and supports distortions in our language about God and about the world, and in the concrete arrangements of our lives together, including in our systems and institutions.

Now, if gender is as important as I have suggested, and if we are still to make the ancient Christian assertion that God is beyond gender because "beyond body, parts, and passions," then names for God which show a preference for one gender over another are simply inappropriate. Indeed, we are actively misnaming God unless we *explicitly* and *clearly* indicate that God is beyond gender, and certainly beyond the way that any particular culture has understood the gender of its human participants. We have generations of traditions (including iconography) which suggest otherwise, and the effects of this must be corrected and transformed.

In our culture, the terms "Father" and "Son" are gendered terms. To deny this is either disingenuous or naive. But to recognize that these terms *are* gendered is not necessarily to say that they must be discarded. There are other options. We can *also* address God using relational terms that are gendered in another way (Mother, for example), *and* that are either not obviously gendered or are gender-inclusive (Creator, Ruler, Savior, and so on). Not to take these steps is to call into question the truthfulness of claims that God is beyond gender.

We need to take another step as well. What any name or descriptive term attempts to convey, I suggest, is the type and quality of relationship involved. Given the diversity of human culture and the plurality of individual experience, no single word is likely to convey any quality, no matter how well-attested that word may be in our collective tradition. When we seek to convey qualities of the divine life and relation with creation, given the figurative nature of all God-language, we most likely need even lengthier descriptions and evocations. This may mean, among other things, that our liturgies will take on greater and greater narrative characteristics and lose some of their terseness.

The point of my opening questions was to provoke us to look at the hidden assumptions about gender that are significant in the discussion of trinitarian formulae. This exercise may have been provocative in another way as well: gender is of such profound importance in our lives that raising questions about it may provoke unease and even fear, and so stimulate resistance. I believe that the presence of resistance in the contemporary discussion is apparent in the trivializing, dismissive, and even pejorative remarks which can be found in even the most scholarly of works arguing against reform of liturgical language about God. Another symptom of resistance is the persistent refusal of many in the church and the academy to consider publicly the claims of womanist, feminist, and other scholars that the texts and traditions of Christianity are profoundly patriarchal and androcentric.

Such resistance should be taken seriously, because it may signal the reaching of limits that do demand recognition and that should compel empathy and compassion. Nevertheless, the significant presence of resistance should not deter us from assessing the role that gender has played in our naming of God. Nor should it prevent us from considering whether we wish that role to continue, or whether modifications are both desirable and possible. The wise course would be to face into the questions and dilemmas with courage, compassion, and willingness to enter into open and frank dialogue, with all the risks that are entailed.

These risks are many, and the stakes are very high. There are numbers of faithful and thoughtful Christians who believe that changes in androcentric liturgical and theological language represent unacceptable, even heretical, changes in the fundamentals of Christian faith. There are also numbers of faithful and thoughtful Christians who are at least as strongly convinced that Christianity's patriarchalism and androcentrism must be overcome if it is, in fact, to be faithful in our time to the Good News of Jesus Christ. The fact that the churches are also dealing with other serious problems, and have been for some time, both clouds vision and saps energy necessary for this particular discussion.

There are, however, some concrete actions that the Episcopal Church can take to provide both reassurance and hope. One is to recognize publicly and officially that the processes of liturgical and institutional reform in which we are involved are of necessity lengthy and important. It is therefore vital that we, as a church, devise generous time frames for the development, use, and evaluation of new materials, and that we recruit the very best and wisest minds and hearts we can find for this work.

Among other things, I suggest that the Standing Liturgical Commission be authorized to proceed with its work on inclusive language for at least another nine to twelve years, with reports to each General Convention, rather than having to convince each General Convention of the importance and merit of its work. Without this kind of time frame, the primary energies in the debate will go toward apologia directed toward legislative processes, and the level of willingness to speak frankly and work creatively will diminish.

It is also necessary that we continue scholarly research and discussion. There are many theological questions and issues at play here, most of which have not been identified and considered overtly. As a systematic theologian, I am convinced that it is only as we allow these issues to be considered that we can imagine creative resolutions to the perennial questions that we face. I also think that such work, when done in public, can provide reassurance both to those who fear that the church is responding to "secular pressure" and to those who long for substantive change.

Finally, I think the development of new texts must continue, and it must do so with even greater boldness and imagination than has been exhibited thus far. While the principles which the Standing Liturgical Commission has adopted are laudable, they must be applied with greater consistency and courage (the latter stimulated by the church's unwavering support for a lengthy period of use and study). That is, we must develop texts that complement the traditional trinitarian names with others which are as explicitly female in gender; we must incorporate female pronouns in reference to God on an equivalent frequency with male pronouns; and we must develop language that stimulates the recognition that human characteristics which are not overtly gendered are nevertheless highly personal. If we do not do this, we are in fact suggesting that there is something more male than female about God, and that would be highly problematic theologically, liturgically, and practically.

These are quite ambitious recommendations, and I am not necessarily optimistic about their prospects, either for adoption or for success. I am, however, convinced that the matter is of very great importance, and we shirk or downplay it at our peril.

How Are We to Name the Trinity in Our Eucharistic Prayers?

Ralph N. *McMichael,* Jr.

The purpose of this paper is to attempt to identify and discuss some of the foundational issues surrounding the question of how we are to name the Trinity in our eucharistic prayers. As will become apparent, I do not think there is one right way to name the Trinity in eucharistic prayers so that we would arrive at the definitive formula of doing this which is then simply repeated in every prayer. The barest knowledge of the history and development of the eucharistic prayer and current prayers throughout the church attest to the diversity of trinitarian language in eucharistic praying. However, in looking at this diversity we might still maintain that there are some common traits of trinitarian language which should be included in any new eucharistic prayers, and that some of the so-called inclusive-language eucharistic prayers stray too far from observed consensus. If this is to be our standard or our methodology for creating new eucharistic prayers, then our task would be to examine all the eucharistic prayers in use in order to identify this assumed consensus on trinitarian language. The implicit rationale for this approach is that the Spirit has led the church to name properly the Trinity in its current prayers, but any new inclusive prayers are a straying from the Spirit because through careful analysis of official prayers we can detect the Spirit's own guidelines for eucharistic praying. I do think that this phenomenological approach to the question of this paper would be of value, but it would not fully answer the question.

The question that I am posing has two dimensions that cannot be considered without reference to each other: how do we address and theologically understand the Trinity, and what is the nature of the eucharistic prayer as theological exposition? In other words, we cannot delve into the complexities of trinitarian theology without regard for the way the church prays this theology. Likewise, we are not to write eucharistic prayers that are theologically illiterate solely because we are driven by a preconceived construct based upon nontheological categories. This necessary and inherent connection between theological understanding and euchological proclamation is to acknowledge the eucharistic prayer as the doxological presentation of the corporate faith of the church. Having said this, I would like to explore the nature of the eucharistic prayer as theological exposition before taking up particular issues of trinitarian theology.

The Eucharistic Prayer as Theological Exposition

The eucharistic prayer is the primary liturgical expression of the church's faith. For the first thousand years of the church's life prior to the total adoption of the Nicene Creed in the Eucharist, the eucharistic prayer was the place where the community's prayer reached the ultimate expression of its life in Christ. This is why the theological content of the prayer has always been considered important and vital to the church's life and understanding of God and the salvific work of Christ. We know that the early church prayed the eucharistic prayer extemporaneously but not *ex nihilo*. That is, there was a basic or traditional structure and content to be followed, but the community through its presider could and did flesh out the prayer, making it always a contemporary prayer. It was not until the fourth century that the eucharistic prayer became overtly prescriptive, a development that corresponded to the church's grappling with trinitarian and christological issues. The prayers themselves became much more theologically developed, reflecting the theological concerns of the church. Although it is outside the scope of this essay, it would be worthwhile to consider these fourth-century anaphoras as theological source since they were written and adopted during a time when classical trinitarian theology was being formulated.

The eucharistic prayer as a theological barometer of the ecclesial times can be seen in Eucharistic Prayer I of Rite One which reflects the theological concern of the Reformation having to do with the relationship between the cross of Christ and the Eucharist. It can also be said that not only does the church shape the theology of the eucharistic prayer, but the eucharistic prayer shapes the theology of the church. The use of the Roman Canon for centuries prior to any official declarations on the presence of Christ in the Eucharist or the sacrifice of the Mass is an example of the eucharistic prayer setting the context for theological development. That there is a theological interplay between the eucharistic prayer and the church's contemporary understanding of God and its life in Christ is something that should be acknowledged and considered in a positive sense.

The interplay or mutuality between the eucharistic prayer and the theological understanding of the church that prays it can be distorted in two ways. First, the nature of the eucharistic prayer as theological exposition is distorted when it is viewed as a series of propositional truths or dogmas. This approach tends toward overly sensitive (paranoid?) assessments of the relative orthodoxy of a given prayer based upon some prior definitive schema of what the prayer should say and how it is to say it. The eucharistic prayer is to have every word "right" and in the "right" order or somehow God will not do what God is supposed to do in the prayer. This approach becomes a linguistic straight jacket which confines the activity of the Spirit to our well-honed objectives. Ultimately, this type of striving for orthodox purity leads not to doxology but to the creation of an idol of our own theological and liturgical technique.

The second way that we can distort the mutual relationship

between the church's faith and the eucharistic prayer is to create prayers that strive to articulate our current (trendy?) theological and ideological preoccupations. Prayers written in this way turn out to be nothing more than euchological mood rings by which we express our narrowly conscribed theological agenda. In other words, this distortion does not create eucharistic prayers that spring from the great tradition of the church and the faith of the church taken as a whole. The result is theme prayers that repetitively drive home the point that is so important to drive home. This same charge can be leveled at theologically driven prayers such as Prayer I of Rite One, the theme being eucharistic sacrifice and the nature of the atonement.

These two ways to distort the nature of the eucharistic prayer as theological exposition provide the boundaries within which to discuss how the prayer is to articulate and shape the corporate faith of the church in a theologically accountable way. Implicit in any approach to the eucharistic prayer and the proclamation of the church's faith is an understanding of the relationship between revelation and experience, or between the great tradition (tradition taken as a whole) and the contemporary situation of the church with its attendant questions and concerns. That is, the first distortion would emphasize a given and definitive, even formulaic, revelation at the expense of current dynamics of the church's life. The second distortion would emphasize present experience and issues of the day as the source of revelation in isolation from the tradition. Both distortions narrowly conceive the interplay between tradition and contemporaneity, or revelation and experience. We are never to consider these realities of the church's life as irreconcilable polarities, but as ever-present dimensions of the ongoing transformation of the church into the fullness of Christ. Eucharistic prayers are always to be traditional and contemporary, faithfully proclaiming God's revelation and reflecting the church's experience of the Spirit.

How then are we to consider the eucharistic prayer as speaking from tradition and to us who gather in the always present moment of the church's life? On the night before his death on the cross, Jesus gave his disciples a way to continue the life that they had shared: he took bread and wine, blessed it with his thanksgiving, shared it with his friends, and exhorted them to do likewise. He exhorted them to "Do this in remembrance of me." The eucharistic prayer is the primary expression of the church's fidelity to this exhortation, and as such, keeping the memory of Jesus becomes its lifeblood and its sustaining bread. Therefore, we should attend to this memory as active and transformative, and we should consider the eucharistic prayer in this way.

In our prevalent West Syrian pattern of eucharistic praying, the exhortation to "Do this in remembrance of me" concludes the thanksgiving section of the prayer which recounts God's acts of salvation culminating in Jesus. It is only after we have remembered what God has done that we begin to ask God to act once again, and we do this with the transitional phrase "remembering...we offer." It is my belief that the role of memory within the eucharistic prayer, and therefore within the church, is the context in which to understand the interplay or mutuality between the prayer as formative tradition and the contemporary life of the church. And I hasten to add that the following discussion of the memorial economy of the eucharistic prayer and of the theological enterprise is not dependent upon an exclusive use of the West Syrian structure. Regardless of the particular structure of a given eucharistic prayer, I think that at the heart of any prayer is keeping the memory of Jesus.

Jesus' exhortation to "Do this in remembrance of me" is our invitation to enter the tradition so that we might speak the tradition anew. Our offerings and petitions in the eucharistic prayer are within the context of our praise of God and our thanksgiving for what God has done in our lives. Our words become self-referent only after our hearts and minds have been shaped by the memory of Jesus which is the enfleshed memory of God. We learn what words are possible when we have kept the memory of the Word that became flesh and showed us that God can speak to us with a human voice. After all, the eucharistic prayer is prayer, and we are moved to pray by the Holy Spirit; however, prayer becomes prayer when it is uttered by a human voice. It is the nature of human voices that they are constituted by particular traits belonging solely to the one who speaks. Tradition as formative of speech becomes prayer when it is spoken by a particular human voice, and the utterance of this voice brings the memory of the tradition into the memory of the present showing us the manifold possibilities for speech in the future. Is this not simply a description of the history of the eucharistic prayer and the theological life of the church?

The Word became flesh so that flesh can speak words that participate in the life of God. The church has never consigned itself simply to repeating the recorded words of Jesus in the Gospels, nor has the church ever been content to articulate its living faith with one set of words to the exclusion of other words. Scripture and tradition are formative for any speech that claims fidelity to the memory of Jesus, but the memory of Jesus still must be spoken with a human voice in order for it to be prayer. Therefore, the memory of Jesus is given its fullest expression when it is spoken by all the voices that make up the church, each having her or his own traits. In fact, scripture and tradition themselves bear witness to the multiplicity of voices speaking the one memory of God. For ultimately, all our voices and all our past and present moments are to speak in such a way that we are led to praise God in the future. Voices that are faithful to the memory of Jesus will always end in doxology, and this is why our eucharistic prayers have always done so.

The economy of the eucharistic prayer is the memory of God definitively offered to us in Jesus, who bids us to keep this memory through speech that issues from our contemporary voice whose *telos* is the praise of God in eternity. This understanding of the eucharistic prayer is the context in which I will now consider how we are to name the Trinity in our eucharistic praying.

Naming the Trinity in Our Eucharistic Praying

The memory of God is trinitarian. The memory of God is forged in personal relationship, and as such it is always a relational memory and never an individual self-contained memory. This means that our words about and to God—our prayer and theological exposition—are spoken within the matrix of relationality and communal life. Since the eucharistic prayer is our being drawn through the keeping of the memory of Jesus into the memory of God, our eucharistic praying will be trinitarian. The question becomes how we are to articulate, or choose the words, to express this inherent trinitarian character. In order to answer this question we are to keep in mind what I said above concerning scripture and tradition and the contemporary voice of prayer in terms of the eucharistic prayer as theological exposition.

It was Karl Rahner who said that the immanent Trinity is the economic Trinity and the economic Trinity is the immanent Trinity (*The Trinity*, p. 22). What this means is that we can never consider the trinitarian nature of God apart from God's relationship to us: theology cannot be separated from soteriology. Therefore, the naming of the Trinity in our eucharistic prayers is not for the purpose of metaphysical musing on the interior life of God, nor is it to be a series of hypostatic hypotheses. Our naming of the Trinity in our eucharistic prayers is for the purpose of drawing us ever deeper into the trinitarian life through praise, thanksgiving, and supplication. We praise, give thanks, and invoke with words that arise from the trinitarian way in which God relates to us, and these words spring from scripture, tradition, and our trinitarian experience of God spoken through the contemporary voice.

Since the memory of God is trinitarian, and therefore relational, our naming of the Trinity will be with words that are relational in character. Relational language for the Trinity found in scripture and tradition become sources for our relational language for God in eucharistic praying because they are normative expressions of the memory of God. But let us not forget, the antithesis of memory, that the relational language found in these sources is multidimensional and that the memory of God is conveyed to us through the communal memories of others. Remembering how God's people or the church has named the Trinity in credal or doctrinal formulation, theological exposition, and prayer does not set aside our own relational memories; instead, we come to knowledge of how our relationships are to lead us into the relational life of the trinitarian God. Therefore, to name the Trinity in our eucharistic prayers is to choose words from the normative expressions of God's memory as this memory is related to us *and* from our contemporary relational language in which we give voice to our life in Christ, in which we pray.

Given my theological understanding of how we are to name the Trinity in our eucharistic prayers, I think that in creating new eucharistic prayers we should always choose the words Father, Son, and Spirit because these are the normative expressions of the memory of God, and to use them is to keep faithfully the memory of Jesus. However, given what I have also said about the multidimensional nature of these normative expressions of God's memory and about our relational language giving voice to the trinitarian nature of God's relationship to us, I think that we should also use other words to name the Trinity in our eucharistic prayers. Some of these words will demonstrate a feminine syntax because our relational life always has a feminine dimension. God's memory is neither male nor female (something often lost on those who push what I call the masculinist agenda); however, we are drawn into the memory of God in relational ways which bear the mark of our relational language—male and female.

In the previous paragraph, I have made two assertions which might seem conflicting: we are to name God as Father, Son, and Spirit in our eucharistic praying, and we can use feminine imagery to speak of God. I would like to expand on these two statements by saying more about the normative memory of God and about the type of eucharistic prayer I have in mind.

Our memory of God, the corporate memory of the church, is normatively expressed and formed by Father, Son, and Holy Spirit. However, this memory tells us that naming God in this way is not to employ synonyms for a male God. The practice of attributing male attributes to God is a distortion of the memory of the church because it strives to say something that the church has wished not to say: God is male. The way to overcome this distortion liturgically is to juxtapose feminine language with our normative symbols.

The church's vocation to keep the memory of Jesus requires vigilance because this memory can, and does, become distorted. This memory belongs to all the baptized and not just to a few self-appointed guardians of memory who invariably define the church's memory in a self-serving way. The memory of Jesus can be disturbing and challenging, and it might lead us to repentance. Why then should we be faithful to the memory of Jesus and to the normative memory of Father, Son, and Spirit so that this memory does not become distorted? Simply put, so that we will not become distorted. Or, so that our present distortions may be transformed into a more adequate expression of the trinitarian life, which is the baptismal life.

Father, Son, and Spirit forms the normative symbol of God in which we are baptized. As such, this symbol never has a univocal meaning nor an equivocal meaning (both are a betrayal of the nature of symbol). Through this symbol we are invited to live into the reality given in the symbol—the very life of the triune God. This living-into-symbol is the process of conversion: we name the Trinity in prayer not so that we can get God right, but rather so that God can make us right. If orthodoxy is not the source of orthopraxis, then "our orthodoxy" is nothing less than a well-conceived apologetic for institutional sin. In other words, the naming of the Trinity is to lead us to live trinitarian lives of loving mutuality between persons who are manifestly equal in the life of God and the church. Having said this, I am not saying that our eucharistic prayers, and our naming of the Trinity within them, are simply chants at a solemn pep rally that when properly shouted inspire us to be trinitarian. Naming the Trinity is not so that we can imitate the Trinity: we name the Trinity so that the Trinity can save us and draw us ever more deeply into God's life. Memory is never imitation; memory is openness to God's salvific disclosure of self.

The type of eucharistic prayer which would adequately express what I have developed thus far is characterized by prolixity. What I mean is that concise theological formulations should be avoided when feminine imagery is incorporated into a eucharistic prayer. Here we are also dealing with the issue of several prayers which vary as to content and structure. A eucharistic assembly may use a variety of eucharistic prayers which, taken as a whole, present a fuller expression of the church's faith than the use of one prayer. However, the practice of a variety of prayers does not mitigate the need for a eucharistic prayer to function as an adequate expression of corporate faith within the eucharistic economy. Therefore, I envision eucharistic prayers such as our present Prayer D, which would employ a catena of images drawn from our memory of God—the memory of Jesus present in our midst. As we name the Trinity in our eucharistic prayers, our memories—female and male—are drawn by the power of the Holy Spirit into the memory of Jesus who presents them to God. Who we are now resides within God's memory, and the life of the Trinity becomes our life.

Session Two: Panel Discussion

Ralph McMichael, Ellen Wondra

**Excerpts from the panel discussion and
response from participants**

Looking at the present Eucharistic Prayer D, we see a model for further development in language. Prayer D is a highly poetic and visual prayer that traces the theology of salvation using a wide variety of imagery. We need to place more emphasis on verbs and less on nouns.

We need as a church to learn how to analyze a prayer. Look at the verbs. When do you give thanks, invoke? Look at the rhythms of prayer. How does a given people bless, give thanks, invoke, intercede? This may lead us to a different kind of structure.

A question addressed to Ralph in regard to his paper: How do we experiment with trinitarian language when we must always come down to Father, Son, and Holy Spirit? Ralph's response: Eucharistic praying that upholds community is not a formula, but primarily a theological expression of church. It does not all have to be nailed down. We don't need to say it all at once in one prayer. Look at eucharistic prayer within the whole Eucharist.

To understand the Trinity is to understand the relational nature of Christian life. Naming the Trinity is to draw us into trinitarian life, not to get it right. Life of the Trinity is relational. The language comes from our relationship with God. Love is at the center of this relationship, of course. Perhaps we don't need to specifically name the Trinity at every occasion. Let that specific naming be balanced with the awareness of the Trinity and the experience of the Trinity lived out in community that can be expressed with a richness of symbol and metaphor. We would never use such non-personal terms as "Creator, Sanctifier, Redeemer," but we can explore the wonder of the relatedness of the Trinity with expansive language that is "anchored" with the traditional naming of the Trinity as Father, Son, and Holy Spirit that is always heard at *some* point or points within the celebration of the liturgy.

Look at the Trinity from different angles. Julian did it with different interlacing triads: God as Father, Mother, Lord—Power, Wisdom, Love; God as nature, ground of our nature, mercy and grace. This is another example of how someone looking at Father, Son, and Holy Spirit can get at the syntax of the structure and articulate different levels of analogy.

As Christians, we live in a trinitarian structure of reality. All that we know about the world around us is one of relationship. The exchange of the Peace at the Eucharist is a highly trinitarian moment. Let's take a more holistic view of the service.

Session Three: Focus Questions

How does culture shape and reshape the language we use in worship out of the ever-evolving life of the people? Some images and metaphors no longer convey meaning to society today, and at the same time society creates new ways we might speak of God that are not a part of our tradition. In other words, how can our language of prayer, which to some extent incarnates our culture, divest itself of unhelpful or dated images, and while rooted in tradition, find itself ever open to what is new?

Dialogue or Disputation: The Character of the Debate about Inclusive Language

Patricia Wilson-Kastner

In the fall of 1969, on a crisp and sunny Iowa day, I sat attentively in a basement classroom in Gilmore Hall while Professor Baird lectured the beginning doctoral students about the perils of sloppy methodology in the study of religion. At the risk of falling into a beginner's pitfall, I suspect that at least some of our discussions about inclusive language would benefit from explicit exploration of the purpose of religious language with respect to religion and society as a whole.

My approach in this paper is not technical or scholarly, but only to raise some questions I think are essential to our present enterprise of exploring the use of inclusive language in our liturgy. Because reality is always far more complex than surface observations might suggest, please consider a thesis which will almost certainly be relevant in discussions of the various responses to the use of inclusive language in the liturgy.

My contention is merely that in the religious community a great deal of argument about inclusive language is not about language or about God, but involves profoundly felt, even if sometimes inadequately articulated, differences of opinion about cultural values and social structures. If there is some truth to this perception, then dialogue about theology may be only a relatively small part of people's real objections to or support of inclusive language.

Religious Language and Its Social Function

Religious language serves a multiplicity of purposes. It expresses profound emotion, conveys information, evokes responses, about humanity's relationship to the divine or the connection of humanity and the world in perspective of the divine. As we use it to communicate, religious language is not disconnected from the rest of the world, nor does it exist in a vacuum apart from the rest of society.

Specialists in the sociology of religion thus for over a century have been reminding us that religion is not a free-floating phenomenon but exists in complex interrelationship with the society as a whole.[1] Especially in a pluralistic society in which different value-systems and religious communities exist, religion and religious language express particular values and assessments of the society as a whole. For instance, the Appalachian Baptist preacher, whose sermons are full of "woe"s pronounced upon the lax and disobedient world of the unsaved and exhortations for the believers to separate themselves from their sinful or negligent neighbors, expresses a judgment about the whole society. Such religious rhetoric serves the purpose of condemning the prevalent values of the society, distancing the religious community from ordinary social practices, and encouraging within the religious community an other-worldly perspective which actively avoids making any changes in the world's social fabric, except to protect the converted from evil.

To take another extreme example, the German Evangelical Church in Germany during the period of the Third Reich acclaimed Hitler as a manifestation of the Holy Spirit and taught that the superiority of Aryan blood was a matter of divine revelation. Such teaching, combined with their active support of Hitler's government, occasioned the Confessing Church's brave critique of them on the basis of the Gospel. The "German Christians" provide one of the clearest modern examples of how a religious system, with its liturgical and theological language, can function as the explicit sacralizer and defender of a government and its social, political, and military ambitions.

Some among us may remember 1963, when the Roman Catholic Church changed the ordinary language of its corporate worship from Latin to the vernacular. I was then a member of a Roman Catholic religious order and a student in a conservative Catholic university in Texas. The lamentations of students and faculty were very clearly about two related but quite distinct issues. The clear concise Latin of Roman worship was being transformed into an aesthetically far less excellent and less doctrinally precise English. But besides the loss of some "beauty of holiness" and a slide into more fuzzy doctrinal standards, another complaint was frequently and eloquently spoken.

If Latin goes, people said, then the language which has held Christendom together for hundreds of years will cease to unify us. Those ideals had been articulated for the twentieth century by Jacques Maritain, T.S. Eliot, and other lesser intellectual lights. Latin, these supporters of the ideal of Christendom argued, has been a symbol and vehicle for the unified cultural ideal based on Christian values of belief in the God of the Bible, humanity's sinfulness and redemption, a common good in civil life, and certain human rights to be respected in all by their very creation as God's children. People from Carlist monarchists to Catholic worker anarchists uttered the same complaint. An important cultural ideal, which may or may not ever be realized in fact, had been irreparably threatened by that liturgical change.

Some of the same arguments have been raised about the changes in Anglican/Episcopal liturgy. Cranmerian English emerged from a high-water mark in English-speaking culture; to lose it, opponents of change allege, is to settle for the norms of an inferior and increasingly antireligious civilization. The language of contemporary Prayer Book revision marks an unhappy change of direction in the church's ministry. Instead of lifting the people of our present confused and fragmented late twentieth-century society up to a common ideal of elevated theology and high culture, we are speaking in *their* words and with their limited sense of the good. At best we may lose much of the challenge and the divine inspiration of the Gospel and the transformed world which is our ideal.

"Inclusive language" is still most widely understood as language speaking about God and the human/Christian community as inclusive of reality as lived and experienced by male and female human beings. The use of inclusive language in the church, as so understood, proclaims that the previous language of worship and the ideal community it reflected and sanctioned, if not sanctified, is at least inadequate to express our vision of God and God's will for the world.

In the previously idealized popular world of non-inclusive, God was visualized and verbally portrayed as a white male, men were the dominant figures named in worship, and maleness and male-related characteristics superior to female ones. Despite objections that high theological and religious culture rejected those views, popular religion and art accepted and promulgated that perspective. That world is now being questioned by calls for inclusive language.[2]

Changes using inclusive language call into question a familiar religious vision and at the same time, and perhaps more disturbingly for some people, a secular and civil ideal of human relationships sanctified by the liturgy. Many opponents of inclusive language would argue that this language is an instrument of radical and undesired social change.[3] The strategy for such change is not direct advocacy of a new Christendom, but presentation of a substantially different ideal of God's purposes for the created order than the replication on earth of a monarchical/hierarchical male-dominated order of heaven. No matter how one accepted that previous ideal, the change in language does in fact, even at its most conservative, represent advocacy of significant change from previously commonly advocated ideals.

Many would argue that these changes are good. Some of us would argue that they are more faithful to classical Christian orthodoxy and social ideals than present noninclusive liturgical language. Nonetheless, the change in language represents a profound threat to many people's sense of social stability and cohesion at a time when they believe that the church ought to be a bastion of social order and stability. These people might best be described as feeling that the church has betrayed them, not just religiously, but by becoming an agent of destruction for the whole world which they value.

So What? I have spent so much time discussing functions of religious language because I want to underscore the deep-seated and often unarticulated anger and frustration of many opponents of inclusive language. They are right in perceiving that liturgical language plays an important role in bolstering or critiquing a society. If one wants to support uncritically a society, either the current society or the society as it is prayed for in the liturgy, then changing liturgical language is an action to be vehemently opposed.

I would not suggest that everyone who is opposed to inclusive language is a mossback conservative, trying to protect the status quo—or a fantasized twelfth-, sixteenth- or nineteenth-century idealized society. However, I would suggest for any further conversations that: 1) the unarticulated and sometimes unconscious connections we make between liturgy and society need to be made explicitly if honest dialogue is to be encouraged; 2) for this reason theological and liturgical dialogue alone about inclusive language is woefully inadequate for the task at hand.

To the end of furthering understanding, if not agreement, I suggest that we be more overt about the multiform functions of language. We may broaden each others' perspectives and gain a deeper appreciation of the motivations people have for taking their varied positions about change in language and in other matters. If we do not broaden our conversations about religious language and its functions, we run the risk of incompleteness, dishonesty, and deception in understanding others and in explaining ourselves.

Religious Language and the Cafeteria Christian

In addition to continued work in exploring the functions of religious language with regard to our relationship to society, we would do well also to look at the religious community using this language, a phenomenon which affects contemporary debates about inclusive language, is increasingly acknowledged in pastoral practice, but, in my opinion, is not often taken adequate account of in discussions of inclusive language. Much of our discussion about inclusive language assumes a religious community with members who range from a virtually fundamentalist orthodox, who would oppose any change in God-language from the present practice as they define it, to very open modern liberals, for whom religious language is changeable at will because our perceptions of God are historically conditioned. Within this range various permutations are included, such as an orthodoxy more open to incorporating various strands of the tradition as well as new developments consonant with scripture.

However, in the churches today, we find that large numbers of members do not make their theological decisions on that sort of basis. One way of describing the situation is to say that many people in churches are uncatechized and unfamiliar with the vast history and contemporary extent of life in the church. At best they are sacramentalized members who have been baptized and know how to receive the sacraments or participate in worship with sincere devotion. Whether they are high or low church, "traditionalist" or "liberal," the common bond is that personal preference determines their allegiance to their belief, practice, or religious patterns of behavior.[4]

"Cafeteria religion" is the somewhat pejorative if picturesque term used today to describe such an approach. The popular press has recently discovered that many younger people interested in religion are returning to religious belief and practice to pick what they like and ignore what they don't like. Easy to identify are the Roman Catholics who go to weekly Mass and use artificial birth control; one can also discover their more conservative counterparts who are faithful to the most Roman observance of the minutiae of the liturgy but ignore or oppose the social teachings of the Roman pontiffs.

One can also find Christians who have Jewish spouses or relatives and go sometimes to church and sometimes to synagogue, or to neither. One can listen to parishioners in the most sedate Episcopal parishes who, behind closed doors, admit that they really don't believe in the doctrine of the creeds or scriptures, but they find the worship beautiful and emotionally satisfying. Their real religious belief centers around spiritualism, reincarnation, and astrology. In other parishes and congregations, the center of emotional attention may for some be a coven or one of the burgeoning twelve-step groups.

My point is not theological or even liturgical analysis, merely to identify substantial numbers of such people who are self-identified members of our church. They, I suggest, do not engage in discussion about inclusive language from the same perspective as official, "high" religion—orthodox, liberal, or in-between—would prefer. Instead, their key assumption is: "I believe and practice what I choose because I choose to believe or practice it." Their allegiance is not to any traditional system of beliefs or practices or any living or even extinct community.

Rather, their loyalty is to themselves as the arbiter if not the source of order and meaning in life. By that I mean that such decisions as what to call God or whether even to participate in church are made out of one's own individual self. Usually, foremost in such judgments are the questions of what makes the individual feel good or secure. The dynamism controlling the person's beliefs and practices is the satisfaction of basic individual needs and desires without any significant reference to a wider religious community than the self. In *Habits of the Heart*, the description of "Sheilaism" is instructive in its brevity:

> Sheila Larson is a young nurse who has received a
> good deal of therapy and describes her faith as
> "Sheilaism." "I believe in God. I'm not a religious

> fanatic. I can't remember the last time I went to
> church. My faith has carried me a long way. It's
> Sheilaism. Just my own little voice....It's just try to
> love yourself and be gentle with yourself. You
> know, I guess, to take care of each other. I think
> He would want us to take care of each other."[5]

What to Do?

Even if I knew how to tackle the complexities of the various social functions of religious language or our contemporary penchant for deciding our own religious belief and practice purely on the basis of what pleases us, there is neither time nor space in this small paper. I would, however, offer some suggestions.

What we see is not always what we get. That is a good methodological beginning. Overtly theological or religious conversation is often about nonreligious issues in addition to or even instead of the articulated religious theme. We can have much more productive dialogues if we are more explicit about how we believe religious language functions and for whom.

Two additional areas seem to me important if we are serious about deepening our conversations about liturgical language in relation to God and our communication with God. The first involves Christian education and the second the practice of prayer.

If most contemporary Christians are not adequately catechized, that is, they do not know the history or practice of the community to which they belong, we may well conclude that education is a crying need for our church. If people have no awareness of the depth and breadth of the scriptures (for instance, if they do not even know where the Gospels are) how can they decide if it is appropriate to use material from the Wisdom tradition in the Eucharist or Offices? If people do not know that for many centuries quite orthodox and mainstream people prayed to Jesus our Mother on the basis of scripture and their experience of God, how can they make informed decisions about (or even fully participate in) liturgical use of prayers addressed to God using maternal imagery?

Of course I am not so naive as to expect that every Episcopalian will or should have an advanced degree in church history and theology, or even that all interpretations of the data of church history will be identical. However, I would think it beneficial for individuals and the community to have a basic awareness of the core of the Christian tradition and enough knowledge to know that the biblical God has many names and epiphanies, recorded right between the covers of the Old and New Testaments. Most people will not know details or even main lines of the church's history, but they can learn in Sunday School and adult class about the different ways Christians have experienced and named God.

The second area of great need is to encourage people in the practice of prayer which is a genuine encounter with God. I am convinced that nothing would do more to free people from the rigidity which asserts that God can be worshiped only under specific formulae, than an encounter with the living God, "I am who I will be." The practice of prayer frees Christians to trust that God's reality is richer than we can ever express and that it is theologically misleading to allow too little of God's reality to be expressed, as happens when language about God is restricted by mere custom or refusal to explore the breadth of scripture and revelation. A refocusing on corporate prayer as encounter with God rather than on simply the words of liturgy might also help us redirect our energies to the search for expressions of God's continuing presence among us, instead of fixating on words isolated from their complex context and broader meanings.

Notes

1. Bronislaw Malinowski, *Magic, Science, and Religion* (Garden City, NY: Doubleday, Anchorbook, 1954), esp. pp. 54-69; Leonel L. Mitchell, *The Meaning of Ritual* (Wilton, CT: Morehouse-Barlow, 1977), pp. 11-35; Robert Bocock, *Ritual in Industrial Society* (London: Geo. Allen & Unwin, 1974), pp. 35-97.

2. Inclusive language may include non-gender-specific language about God, an effort to balance gender-related and non-gender-related language about God, language which explicitly advocates a multicultural human society, as well as other variations. The term "inclusive language" for any particular writer or speaker may include more or less than those aspects listed here. "Inclusive language" is not a univocal term.

3. William Oddie, *What Will Happen to God?* (London: SPCK, 1984).

4. Mark Searle, "Private Religion, Individualistic Society, and Common Worship," in *Liturgy and Spirituality in Context*, ed. Eleanor Bernstein (Collegeville, MN: Liturgical Press, 1990), pp. 27-46; W.C. Roof & W. McKinney, *American Mainline Religion: Its Changing Shape and Future* (New Brunswick NJ: Rutgers, 1987), pp. 148-185; Robert Bellah, et al., *Habits of the Heart* (New York: Harper and Row, 1985), esp. pp. 142-163.

5. *Habits of the Heart*, p. 221.

Language Shaped and Shaping

Juan M.C. Oliver

The current interest in the way our representations of the world and of God are affected by our understanding of gender has been accompanied—not always in tandem—by a concurrent concern with the relationship between liturgy and culture. Thus while some of us have been paying attention to how our liturgy is gender-bound, others have studied it in relation to its surrounding culture. It is this second angle that I wish to explore here, concentrating less on matters of gender than on the ways in which liturgical language is formed by—and in turn forms—culture.

I will not address the issue from an aesthetician's or a poet's point of view; I am not interested at this moment in how language is shaped by the artist or in language as a medium of expression for the individual writer. This is an important question to be addressed by members of liturgical drafting committees, for they must produce language that is at once contemporary, exalted and artful.

However, I mean to address the phenomenon of liturgical language in relation to culture. This sounds like a big issue, and it is, but we must face it as it involves a wider relationship, one at the heart of our discussion: the relationship between culture and ritual. I suspect that this relationship lies at the core of our growing concern about the connections between liturgy and justice, between "orthodoxy" and "orthopraxis."

Culture and the Work of Justice

It seems strange to bring justice into the conversation at this point. How can ritual bring about social change towards a more just society? Ritual is by nature conservative—a way of preserving and propagating culture from generation to generation. Yet rituals themselves change, sometimes in ritual fashion, as Catherine Bell has suggested.[1]

Our liturgical language may need to change if our right praise (*orthodoxia*) is to lead us into right doing (*orthopraxis*). Many of us may get there by God's grace, perhaps involving right praise to some extent, but usually this happens only because we have been so acculturated to the language of our tradition that we are able to translate it with little effort into plain English and acts of justice. Our liturgical language does not prompt us to acts of justice, not because it is perverse or perverted, but because the language that we use to speak about the great deeds of God is no longer used by our culture to discuss sacred and transcendent things.

Additionally, what we usually mean by orthodoxy does not stem from this sense of the relationship between right praise and right doing. It stems, rather, from an understanding of orthodoxy that sees belief as a set of statements rather than as ritual action. This leads to discussions about the content of dogmatic statements without reference to their liturgical origins or to their connection to the historical or contemporary Christian assembly at prayer. As a result, orthodoxy understood in this disembodied way fails to proclaim a *felt* vision of a just world, concentrating instead on a vision *understood* and passing the responsibility for communicating the guts of the vision to the preacher who is entrusted with the task of applying theological concepts to practical issues.

It may be suggested that any ritual community such as ours must develop and employ its own language to speak of its own experience of the sacred. This is unquestionable to some extent. But we must also employ the broader language of our culture to speak about our experience if it is to be communicated to anyone outside our circle. Instead, our liturgical language is becoming so specialized that it must be translated into plain English in order for the average person to understand what we are saying. I will label this "disinculturated language."

By and large, we employ such language in our liturgy with one of two assumptions: either the language really does not have to be understood or the persons involved in the rite have been initiated into its use. In fact, the second assumption, the need for initiation, is sometimes heard among people advocating for newcomer's programs and even the catechumenate. For them catechesis is the process of explaining our lore to potential new members.

But true catechesis is not a matter of translating a text for the ritually naive. It is rather the process of conversion in response to God's initiative. The time spent explaining our specialized language might be better spent with the catechumen listening to ways in which God is transforming his or her life and discerning ways in which to cooperate with God. But this cannot take place as long as we have to spend most of our time explaining what we mean.

What Is Constructed May Be Changed

In the last twenty-five years or so culture has come to be understood as a thing constructed and thus capable of change. Before, we considered culture as an essence: a communal identity surviving immutable through changes in time and space. But now, in our deconstructivist climate, we refer to it as the social construction of reality.

Thus culture is no longer seen as an inanimate object; rather, like a growing, living thing, it forms and propagates itself, changes, adapts and dies. Language and ritual, the two aspects that bring together the participants in the Consultation on Language and Liturgy, are major ways in which culture grows, adapts, changes and propagates itself.

The Theology of Inculturation

This insight, that a culture is not a static thing but a reality capable of undergoing change, lies behind the recently coined term, *inculturation.* Coined in the early 1960s by several theologians, the term refers to:

the incarnation of the Christian life and of the
Christian message in a particular cultural context
in such a way that this experience not only finds
expression through elements proper to the culture
in question (this alone would be no more than a
superficial adaptation) but becomes a principle that
animates, directs and unifies that culture, transforming it and remaking it so as to bring about a
"new creation."[2]

Anscar Chupungco has defined inculturation as "the process
whereby the texts and rites used in worship by the local church are
so inserted in the framework of culture that they absorb its
thought, language, and ritual patterns."[3]

A theology of inculturation has as one of its major points of
departure the Incarnation of God in human history. But a theology of the incarnation which presents it only as the intervention of
God "from above," while stressing the Word's own incarnation
into first-century Jewish life and thought, his need of cultures in
order to spread the Gospel, and his particular relationships with
members of other cultures, nevertheless gives the impression that
there is nothing of value in the culture apart from what is brought
to it by Christ. As Shorter notes, "the understanding of inculturation as an ongoing dialogue between gospel and culture is more or
less overlooked."[4]

However, this view of the Incarnation entirely "from above"
does not do justice to another aspect of christology: the presence,
at the core of creation, of the Word in whom all things were made.
It is this presence of the Logos in cultures which opens up the possibility of an intercultural dialogue between Gospel and cultures,
in which the culture is a dynamic element in relation to the Gospel
and not a mere passive recipient of it.

The Christ who took human flesh is the Word in
whom all has been created. This means that he is at
the heart of all human cultures, that he is responsi-

ble for all that is good in them and that he makes
them vehicles of salvation.[5]

The incarnation of the church in specific cultures is not the
same thing as the assimilation of the church into a cultural system to give it divine corroboration. There is a redemptive agenda
behind inculturation; otherwise, inculturation would not mean
transformation of the culture, only cooptation of the Gospel by
the culture.

The Inculturation of Liturgical Language

If the liturgy is, as Yves Congar has said, "the epiphany of the
Church,"[6] it follows that the inculturation of the liturgy is central
to the manifestation of the church not only to itself but to the
world. I turn now to several more specific aspects of liturgical
inculturation.

Vatican II provided, in its Constitution on the Sacred Liturgy,
for a certain level of adaptation:

> Provided that the substantial unity of the Roman
> rite is preserved, provision shall be made, when
> revising the liturgical books, for legitimate varia-
> tions and adaptations to different groups, regions,
> and peoples, especially in mission countries.[7]

However, this adaptation of the Roman rite envisioned by the
Council Fathers does not go far enough in addressing the funda-
mental cultural spirit characteristic of specific cultures, a spirit
which generates the externals of music, color, instrumentation, etc.
Writing about the inculturation of the liturgy in Africa, E.
Elochukwu Uzukwu suggests:

> It is only when the liturgist starts to grapple with
> the fundamental perception of the universe by vari-
> ous African peoples, their understanding of the life
> of man lived in dynamic relation to ancestors, to
> good and evil spirits, to good and evil people, to
> the physical universe and God embodied in myth

and ritual; only when this perception of the universe is taken seriously and its role as a problem-solving mechanism in the real African universe...is seen *dia-loguing* and not *duo-loguing* with a critiqued and living, thereby evolving, Jewish-Christian tradition...do we have an African liturgy in the making.[8]

Multiculturalism in the Episcopal Church

Monocultural understandings of reality are already out-of-date and in many ways obsolete. This may be due to the fact that in our multicultural experience cultures do not exist side by side, each hermetically sealed from the other, but like the components of the tofu burrito and Coke I just had for lunch, are constantly affecting and erupting inside each other's domain. The alien is within us, and an Episcopal Church which sees itself as monocultural or even monolingual is seriously deluding itself.

Gone are the days when we could afford to construct reality in monocultural terms. Social constructions of reality which insist on doing this today may still survive, but they will be provincial, specialized and ultimately disconnected. For the simple truth that everyone feels in their bones is that reality is not simply white and Anglo-Saxon; it is in fact multiracial and cross-cultural, a mishmash of things and traditions, a collage of details, not always well integrated or compatible. "The way things are" is many ways.

This awareness of the multicultural dimensions of our experience has brought with it a growing sensitivity among Anglo-Saxon Episcopalians towards other cultures. This is perhaps the most important development in the Episcopal Church in recent years, second only to our sensitivity to the role of gender and sexuality in the construction of reality. It would be interesting, but outside our scope, to reflect on the connections between cultural and gender sensitivity in the church.

Our newfound cultural sensitivity is making us aware of the goodness of the other cultures. We find the exotic menu, the charming mannerism, the rare anthropological discovery, the "naive" native artifact purer and better than our own Anglo menus, mannerisms, discoveries and art. We venerate the noble savage in the alien culture, but find only Cain in our own, whereas the truth of the matter is that we find both Cain and the noble savage in all cultures.

But who will dare critique the foreigner? What Spaniard today would dare speak of the sins of the Aztec? What Anglo-Saxon American would dare speak of the sins of African Americans? We share a benevolent disposition (perhaps masking our terror/fascination) towards foreign cultures, best exemplified by Star Trek's prime imperative not to interfere with the development of alien forms of life.

It must be admitted that most of us would rather live with Captain Picard than with the Great Inquisitor. We want to allow the other his or her own autonomy and freedom, and we are providentially willing to look away from his or her fallenness. As a result you see paeans to other cultures such as mine (Latino) which make no mention of our structural evidences of sin: machismo, homophobia, misogyny, family violence. Our hunger for the noble savage is such that we often hire for positions of responsibility incompetent "ethnics" who would never be hired for those positions by their own people, or we excuse behaviors in members of ethnic minorities which their own constituencies would not tolerate.

The obverse is also true. We tend to see only the ills of our own "American" culture, even denying at times that Americans have a culture at all.

Uzukwu's understanding of the work of inculturation as inseparably related to a culture's fundamental perception of the universe lies behind the work of the Standing Liturgical Commission's Subcommittee on the Inculturation of the Liturgy in African-American, Hispanic, Asian, Native-American and Anglo-Saxon congregations—an attempt to apply inculturation theory to the area of liturgy.

Uzukwu distinguishes between hidden and systematic creativity in the work of liturgical inculturation. Hidden creativity is found in the music, hymnody, readings and homilies, art and architecture of African churches, even churches with otherwise markedly "Roman" liturgies. However, he points out that these attempts are "mere adaptations which satisfy immediate cravings" and lack "the space to let go of their primitive dynamism which could transform the structure." Systematic creativity, on the other hand, springs from a process of theological reflection by the local church deepening "its apprehension of the Christ-event through courageous and soul-searching reflection on its faith experience."[9] This reflection leads to the embodiment, in cult, of the conversion experience of the local church in its own cultural context. Systematic creativity is more a matter of discovering and expressing the identity and mission of the local church in a given cultural milieu and less the application of cultural expressions onto an otherwise "Anglican" or "Roman" liturgy.

Assuming that systematic creativity is the goal of liturgical inculturation and that mere adaptation is at best a remedial, temporary step, a procedural question may be asked: How might the inculturation of liturgical language take place? The question immediately leads to another: What is the context for the inculturation of liturgical language in contemporary Anglo-Saxon American congregations?

The Interplay of Culture and Language

Culture shapes language. Language is a cultural artifact, a production of the culture. For this reason a literal translation of a text is never accurate. The conceptual framework, the web of associations, the sound and feel of the language in the body of speaker or listener, all these are culture-specific. The Spanish word *mesa,* for example, may be translated as "table," but in the process we lose the association with a large mountain with a flat top. "Table," in turn, can be associated with underground water, which is untranslatable into *mesa*. Thus translations are always at best partial, and the old saying always holds true: the translator is a traitor. A language is only truly at home in its own culture and only *really* makes sense in that cultural context. As a result a literal translation is not always either accurate or desirable.

Language shapes culture. The influence goes both ways. As a formative element in human development, language also shapes culture. First, language serves culture by passing it on from generation to generation. Word associations and attitudes are transmitted across time and place, giving culture its huge reach and elasticity. But language can also transform culture. When a parishioner insists on saying "she" every time we say "he" about God, the parishioner's speech is effecting a change in the church subculture. The change may be a decision to investigate the use of inclusive language, or a decision to ban it, or a decision to shun the parishioner; in any case, the person's speech is an event which may not be ignored, particularly as it is a ritual change introduced ritually.

To sum up, cultures shape their artifacts, such as language, but are in turn propagated and shaped across time and space through the medium of an artifact such as language.

The same may be said of ritual. It is an expression or manifestation of a given cultural group, imprinting the participants with a particular vision of the world: an ethos and world view. But like language, ritual also shapes culture. Therefore ritual language is in a particularly privileged position both to preserve culture and to change it. In fact, it is probably this insight—that ritual language is both an outward expression and a formative cause of culture—which lies at the foundation of our interest in inclusive, nonsexist language. We are ultimately interested in supporting our culture in its transition away from a construction generated to support patriarchy and its privileges and instead beginning to construct something which favors and values a broader understanding of humanity.

At the same time we are more aware than ever that the liturgy is a thing constructed. One of the great achievements of the liturgical movement in this century has been the development of an historical understanding of liturgy as related to its context. Like dogma, the liturgy is understood today as a social construction necessarily affected by contextual sociopolitical, economic and other factors, and no longer as a static deposit of worship given once for all by Jesus at the Last Supper. As a result, liturgical forms may be examined in relation to the contextual factors surrounding them and adapted or reformed so as to serve the same structural purpose without preserving the actual liturgical form. So, for example, the old Introit Psalm is today replaced by a rubric in the 1979 Prayer Book indicating the singing of the *Gloria in excelsis* or "other song of praise." Whether Introit, *Gloria* or hymn, the structural need to bring the people together in song is served.

The benevolence of Anglo-Saxon Americans towards other cultures that I mentioned above is useful. Thanks to it we may begin to experiment with truly ethnic forms of liturgy, encouraging experimental sites to develop liturgical language, music, and spatial arrangements as they see fit, assisted by consultants as necessary but encouraged to be as ethnically authentic as possible.

Inculturation of English as a Liturgical Language

The average Anglo-Saxon reader would, I think, welcome the idea until it is applied to Anglo-Saxon ethnicity with questions such as: Is the language of the liturgy truly American? How does the language of the liturgy in English present our vision of the Dominion of God? Is that vision American? That is, to what extent is the language of our English liturgies, for example, imbued with egalitarianism, with a certain measure of individualism, with a sense of the land as a limitless blessing?

Our culture is in the middle of a revolution reaching down into its unconscious foundations. Deconstructivist critique is showing us that what we consider to be "common sense" and "the way things are" is a convention generated to order society in such a way as to value and favor some at the expense of others. This is, in a sense, a cultural law: something is always being raised and praised at the expense of something else being therefore lowered and despised.

Feminist critique has been at the forefront of this deconstruction of patriarchy. But our work as worshiping congregations may not stop here. We are called to present, for our own perception and others, a felt sense of a different world order.

This means that the liturgical community must have a sense, however inchoate, of the Dominion of God as it might be lived out in social, economic, and political ways. The liturgy is the acting out of this Dominion of God in perceptible ways—language, choreography, visuals, etc.—so that it may be seen and heard by us. In the process of revealing this vision, Christian ritual forms us in it. We are immersed in a different world view communicated in the ritual action itself through the ordering of bodies in space and time. In this way a set of power relations is generated and maintained.

For our purposes here, we want to pay attention to how our ritual involves our bodies in relation to language. We gather in ritual to speak, sing, read and listen. How are these actions formative? Into what are the actions forming us? To what extent is the rhetorical shape of our ritual language forming us into something? To what extent are our linguistic assumptions helping to propagate an ethos and world view? Is what we are forming an anachronism?

Louis Weil is fond of making a distinction between mystery and mystification. The liturgy of Christians is a manifestation or proclamation of the paschal mystery, not its obfuscation. Liturgy engages mystery, the endlessness of God's mercy towards us, by bringing us to that pond to drink, not by giving us a liturgical crossword puzzle that completed, reads, "There is a wideness to God's mercy but we are not showing it to you or telling you where it is or how to get there." Instead, the liturgy should present, in seen, heard and felt ways, our shared vision in a language immediately accessible to those present.

Why don't we do this? Why do we insist on using theological concepts which are not current in the culture in which we find ourselves? One snide possibility is that we like words that mean nothing because they enable us to fill their blanks with our own ideas. A phrase such as "the Holy Gospel of our Lord Jesus Christ" can be heard as meaning many things:

a. the untouchable book containing the biography of our absolute authority, Jesus (last name:) Christ;

b. the sacred book containing what you have to believe about a man people worship as God, Jesus (last name:) Christ;

c. the wonderful Good News about our guru, Jesus (last name:) Christ;

d. the healing good news of (not about) our leader, Jesus the Chosen of God.

Perhaps the last meaning begins to approximate what the Greek means. Why are we so loath to say what we mean? Perhaps we do not know what we mean. Perhaps our theological language has developed over the centuries as a series of glyphs which in fact have little or no inherent meaning, so that the phrase "The Holy Gospel..." is always in need of interpretation.

I suspect our mystifying language serves a purpose. It keeps us under the impression that we are having a religious experience and away from any concrete meaning in relation to righteousness or justice. Perhaps this stems from the American idea that righteousness is individual and that only individuals can make moral claims, and then only about and for themselves. If this is true, then our ritual language, if it were to mean anything concrete, would have to be solipsistic. Each of us would have to write our own Book of Common Prayer, betraying its title in the process. So I suspect that the only way in which we can have common prayer in this culture is to keep its language vague, since your average collection of people in this culture is loath to make any commonly shared statements about praxis. And without a shared vision of praxis, there cannot be a right praise. How are we to make present what is absent (in the past) to bring into the present what is absent (in the future)? This is the assembly's imaginative work, dreaming the Dominion of God into being. But for this to happen liturgical language must be transparent. At bottom we might ask ourselves: Does knowing that language shapes how we value things move us to change language so that we may value differently?

The inclusivity of our liturgical language is not simply an aesthetic issue (I doubt there is ever a merely aesthetic issue without ethical and political reverberations). The inclusivity of our language is an ethical issue; it deals with the good and evil aspects of our language, seeking to redeem it from its bondage to a power structure and releasing and empowering it to support and form a different version of reality.

In this sense a redeemed language is sacramental. Suffused, like bread and wine, with the Spirit, this language communicates and makes present a reality not yet here: God's reign. It does this not by pointing at it from a distance but by bringing it near, so that, for example, the coming world of gender equality can be heard and spoken now. The inclusivity of our language is essential to its being sacramentally efficacious.

This brings me to my second point: underlying the challenge of inclusive language there is a deeper, broader problem with our language. The liturgical language of the Episcopal Church is increasingly useless. I put it this way to shock you into waking up to the fact that you and I have undergone a long and very subtle process of indoctrination and initiation in the use of our language—sexist or not, that is not my point; and that this language that we are so adept at wielding is increasingly shared by only a precious few people.

If this is true, even after all the Episcopal churches in the country switch to nonsexist language, they will still be emptying out. Let me explain. There are increasing numbers of people with good spiritual intentions who cannot handle commonplace Christian concepts like: Creation, Fall, Sin, Forgiveness, Salvation,

Atonement, Grace (except as graciousness in the sense of polite kindness) and so on. It is not that they disagree with these concepts. It is much worse. The concepts are at best meaningless, and at worst they imply an understanding of God which is utterly uninteresting and undesirable to these people, an understanding of God and how God acts that they find deeply suspect, an understanding of God invested in concepts of law, obedience, power and rebellion. They are suspicious of this God. They find such a God undesirable. And what good can an undesirable God be?

In the sixties we began to lose members as a denomination. I am not sure to what extent these were actual losses or losses by attrition; perhaps people were dying and no new members were joining. Additionally, the societal expectation of church membership for all Americans vanished, without our noticing that the strongest evangelistic arm of Christianity—the culture itself—had undergone a profound shift.

Now I constantly meet people—usually under thirty—who do not have a clue as to what Christianity is. They rely on the pronouncements of televangelists to develop a sense of what it is that we believe. Since we Episcopalians share the same theological language with televangelists, these young people walk into our churches innocently and every suspicion that they have about Christianity is confirmed. I often ask them to mark the service sheet whenever they find something objectionable or puzzling. Allow me to give some examples:

1. Sexist language. Educated young people in urban areas are looking out for patriarchy everywhere, and they do not like it when they see it. Do not tell me that "men" means "all humans"; it doesn't today. You are dating yourself.

2. *Gloria in excelsis.* "Only Son of the Father" is unacceptable; there are many children of God (yes, I know, by adoption; but the casual visitor hasn't heard the Gospel yet, so he or she does not know this). "You alone are the Holy One" is heard in a triumphal tone, intolerant of other religions.

3. "Lord have mercy." This can be heard by people who are in touch with their vulnerability and neediness, but a lot of young urban people do not see any need for God to have mercy on them. Of course they live in denial! But additional imputation of guilt will never help them to relax into conversion and forgiveness. (Oops! I have slipped into *our* language; I mean blaming them will never help them to relax into walking into a new mindset and accepting unconditional love. Hokey? Our language sounds worse to them.)

4. "The Holy Gospel of our Lord Jesus Christ according to..." This is a phrase written in code. In their language, it may go something like: "The Great Good News of our Teacher? Master? Jesus, the Chosen, according to..." (they may balk at Teacher, Master and Chosen until shown that baptism reveals *their* magistery, authority and election).

5. The Creed. "Creed" means to them "What I believe." They have no conception of the communal basis of faith or why we would want to say "WE believe." By and large, they understand the theological constructs of the Creed literally. Occasionally a person will make it clear that it is the very idea of a creed that they have a problem with. These people would rather have as many creeds as there are congregants.

6. Confession. There are several problems with this text. First, the language of sin, repentance and pardon seems archaic, almost quaint. Second, people have sometimes asked me if they must confess their sins to be pardoned by God. The obvious New Testament answer is NO. Additionally, we need to discover how modern Americans express regret over not being perfect, own responsibility for our actions, and receive forgiveness and unconditional love from God regardless of whether we confess or not.

Please, let us not call for more catechesis to address these issues. True catechesis is accompanying someone on the road of conversion as they respond to God's word resounding in their ear.

Catechesis is not didacticism or explanation. It is not instructed liturgies (a clear evidence that the liturgy is sick, the glass dirty, the icon opaque). Translating theological concepts into plain English in a classroom before the Sunday liturgy is not true catechesis. For the word of God truly to resound in the learner's ear it must be spoken in plain language by and within the liturgy, else it cannot be news, let alone Good News. Due to this the entire liturgy must be understood as a homiletic event. And when seen in this light, it needs to be subjected to the same rigorous tests to which any preacher would submit.

We are far, far from Pentecost morning, when "Parthians, Medes, Elamites; inhabitants of Mesopatamia, of Judaea and Cappadocia, of Pontus and Asia, of Phrygia and Pamphylia, of Egypt and the districts of Libya around Cyrene, visitors from Rome, both Jews and proselytes, Cretans and Arabs; [said] we hear them [the disciples] telling in our own tongues the great things God has done" (Acts 2:9-11, New English Bible). Let's begin to move towards that Sunday morning when people will say of us, in amazement: "But these are Christians, aren't they, these speakers? How is it then that we hear them, each of us in our own vocabulary? Yuppies, gays, feminists, inhabitants of all Ecotopia, of college dorms and executive dining rooms; of New Jersey and California; of Kansas and Utah; of Boston and Los Angeles; of Shreveport and the parishes of Louisiana; visitors from Europe, both Christian and unbaptized, neo-pagans and fundamentalists, we hear them telling in our own manner the great things that God has done."

Notes

1. On ritual as an agent of change and transformation, see Catherine Bell, "Ritual Change and Changing Rituals," *Worship 63* (1989): 31-41, and Tom F. Driver, *The Magic of Ritual* (San Francisco: Harper, 1991), pp. 166-191.

2. Pedro Arrupe, S.J., "Letter to the Whole Society on

Inculturation," in *Other Apostolates Today: Selected Letters of Pedro Arrupe, S.J.*, ed. J. Aixala, Vol 33, pp. 172-181.

3. Anscar Chupungco, O.S.B., *Liturgies of the Future: The Process and Methods of Inculturation* (New York: Paulist Press, 1989), p. 29.

4. Aylward Shorter, *Toward a Theology of Inculturation* (Maryknoll, N.Y.: Orbis Books, 1988), p. 81.

5. Ibid., p. 78.

6. Cited by E. Elochukwu Uzukwu, "Liturgy: Truly Christian, Truly African," *Spearhead*, No. 74 (Dec. 1987), p. 29.

7. Second Vatican Council, *Constitution on the Sacred Liturgy*, par 38.

8. Uzukwu, pp. 30-31.

9. Ibid., pp. 36-37.

Bibliography

Aune, Michael B. "Worship in an Age of Subjectivism Revisited." *Worship* 65 (1991): 224-38.

Arrupe, Pedro, S.J. "Letter to the Whole Society on Inculturation." In *Other Apostolates Today: Selected Letters and Addresses of Pedro Arrupe, S.J.* Edited by J. Aixala. Vol. 33, pp. 172-181.

Azevedo, Marcello De Carvalho, S.J. *Inculturation and the Challenges of Modernity.* Rome: Gregorian University, 1982.

Chupungco, Anscar, O.S.B. *Liturgies of the Future: The Process and Methods of Inculturation.* New York: Paulist Press, 1989.

_____. *Cultural Adaptation of the Liturgy.* New York: Paulist Press, 1982.

Empereur, James, S.J. *Exploring the Sacred.* Washington, D.C.: Pastoral Press, 1987.

Hoffman, Lawrence A. *Beyond the Text: A Holistic Approach to Liturgy.* Bloomington, IN: Indiana University Press, 1989.

Langer, Suzanne. *Feeling and Form.* New York: Charles Scribner's Sons, 1953.

Power, David N. *Culture and Theology.* Washington, D.C.: Pastoral Press, 1990.

Schineller, Peter, S.J. *A Handbook on Inculturation.* New York: Paulist Press, 1990.

Shorter, Aylward. *Toward a Theology of Inculturation.* Maryknoll, N.Y.: Orbis Books, 1988.

Smith, Jonathan Z. *To Take Place: Toward Theory in Ritual.* Chicago: University of Chicago Press, 1987.

Uzukwu, E. Elochukwu. "Liturgy: Truly Christian, Truly African." *Spearhead,* No. 74, Dec. 1987.

Session 3: Panel Discussion

Juan Oliver, Frank Griswold, Patricia Wilson-Kastner

Excerpts from the panel discussion

The panelists described the context in which they did ministry.

Three churches Juan has served have these characteristics in common: There is a suspicion of Christianity among people he deals with every day. To walk into a Christian church is to give in to the patriarchy and authoritarian nature of the world, people feel. Christianity has lost whatever good p.r. it had. The high profile of the fundamentalists has contributed to this. Christianity is seen as something we have outgrown. People are interested in the self and in community, but only the immediate community. What they don't experience doesn't exist. Spirituality is really big now, but what they mean by spirituality is picking at your feelings, and the strange warmings of the heart. Spirituality is something very much my own and cannot really be shared. Obedience does not sell. How do we proclaim something to these people if we are perceived as the enemy and the oppressor?

Patricia Wilson-Kastner is rector of a parish in Brooklyn, New York. To say that the parish is multicultural is to understate the reality of the Brooklyn area. The parish has a long history of social action. It is one block from city hall, which may help to explain the immense concern for outreach to the community. Race and sexual orientation are not issues in determining level of acceptance by the parish, but education and professional status are. Large African and Caribbean communities exist around the church building so there is a mix of cultures. The liturgical tastes extend from those who want to use Rite I to those who want to use supplemental texts and stand around the altar. The basic issue Patricia deals with is the nature of the community that is the parish. People come and stay because they want acceptance and belonging. Most of them have been marginalized for some reason or another, and they want a place to come and be accepted for who they are. They come seeking hope. New York City seems ungovernable and people want the community to work. They are tired of the drugs and the crime and the homelessness. People want to believe that there is something that can be better. There is no shared culture or values. Imagination and ability to empathize are squashed in the schools. The need for catechesis is crucial, because we need to give people a sense of belonging and acceptance. They need the practice of prayer and a personal encounter with God.

Frank Griswold's story of a Thanksgiving dinner is his way of getting at an understanding of cultural sensitivity. The Griswolds were invited for Thanksgiving dinner at the home of a rural New Hampshire family who went out of their way to provide things at the dinner they felt an urban Chicago couple would appreciate. A plate full of chicken livers along with newly purchased wine glasses and the sharing of a diary that helped the Griswolds appreciate some of the family traditions became for Frank a model of liturgy. What is the quality of welcome in this place? What makes people feel at home? How is scripture proclaimed? Does it fit the community? How are people hearing the scripture out of the experience they bring to the text? Is the eucharistic prayer expressing the life of the parish? What might be authentic liturgy for a parish may strike an outsider negatively. How does this community play? Am I flexible or free enough to enter into how they play even if it is a game that I do not understand?

Frank is delighted and disturbed by how incarnate everything is in the parishes. "This is how we do things here," the people are saying. We have taken our culture and woven it into the BCP. Everyone sees themselves as normative with no larger sense of community. The job of bishop and priest is to remind people that they are part of the whole church and to point out again and again the common things that hold us together as Christians. The notions of Jesus are so different. Parish liturgies are shaped by the eccentric embellishments of the community, and the liturgy does not challenge the people with the power of the Gospel.

Affirming culture in an imaginative way does not seem to take place. The traditions of Hispanic, African American, Caribbean, bump up against Anglican tradition, but the varied cultures do not really inform liturgy. The community expresses its uniqueness in other ways, but not liturgically. There is often a lack of imagination. Even within the Prayers of the People there is no acknowledgment of the needs of the larger world.

Juan wants to introduce newcomers and outsiders to the church's story, but they will not hear it if it does not fit in with their lives in some way. We must begin with their story, otherwise they are lost. Traditional words of sin, redemption, salvation have no connection with where they are. What they mean by sin is not what we are talking about. Sin for them is unforgivable. Most of the people in his parishes have grown up without church. They are real pagans, and there is no connection at all to the church or the language of the church. Once they have a sense of their own spirituality and story then they can accept tradition. If liturgy is not going to be simply apologetics, then we need to find another form of worship for those who are not churched.

What does a faithful or converted person look like? Someone who is faithful, who meets with other faithful people regularly and has opted for the Christian tradition. Someone who has made a commitment to Christianity and who follows Jesus. A faithful person should be able to answer the question of what their ministry is in light of the baptismal covenant and see the relevance of that ministry in their everyday lives. Faithful people will discover that relevance as they meet together to discover the context of their ministry, as they share their struggle to be faithful and make connections with the faith. A faithful follower of Jesus realizes that we all must be continually converted.

Session Four: Focus Questions

What is it we want to say to each other as this consultation draws to a close?

What do we want to say specifically to the Standing Liturgical Commission as a result of our participation in this consultation?

Session Four: Plenary Discussion

We need to look at this process over a longer period of time than the three years between General Conventions. Can we think in terms of ten to fifteen years with general authorization to continue research, experimentation and evaluation? It might be helpful to work with specific congregations at the "grassroots" level over a long period of time so that the congregations could develop liturgical texts growing out of their worship life. These texts and others produced by the Standing Liturgical Commission would be used and evaluated both by the congregation and by theologians and others who could evaluate the texts in the light of tradition.

Supplemental Liturgical Materials includes revised forms for "An Order for Celebrating the Holy Eucharist" to encourage congregations to develop their own eucharistic prayers ["An Order for Celebrating the Holy Eucharist"—sometimes referred to as "Rite Three"—can only be used where there is "careful preparation by the Priest and other participants" and when the celebration is not "at the principal Sunday or weekly celebration of the Holy Eucharist"].[1] Of course, the provisions for writing liturgical texts for celebrating the Eucharist at informal occasions have been available to us since the authorization of the present Prayer Book, but this flexibility is all too often overlooked. Let us encourage the use of "An Order for Celebrating the Holy Eucharist" so that texts arise more naturally out of the life of faithful congregations. Eucharistic Prayer C came into the Prayer Book from frequent informal use and was finally adapted and accepted as one of the official prayers in the 1979 Book of Common Prayer. The adapted forms for "An Order for Celebrating the Holy Eucharist" were included in *Supplemental Liturgical Materials* with this in mind, but we have little evidence that congregations have taken advantage of the provision.

We must be aware that people who lived through the adoption of the present Prayer Book often resist the thought of changing the Prayer Book again, even though the reasons they accepted for change twenty years ago may still be valid today. Some of the feelings come from the satisfaction of having their own Hymnal and Prayer Book in hand once more. We need to be aware of their feelings and concerns. On the other hand, there are lots of people who are not in church today who might become a part of the church tomorrow if some of what we have talked about here came about.

I dream of a church being comfortable with its diversity. On the one hand we need to respond to those who are uncomfortable with any thought of change, but at the same time we are called to be responsive to people who feel alienated by the worship of the church in its present form. Perhaps some of the diverse needs of people can be met if we realize that small group worship experiences can answer the need to reach out and experiment while the worship of the gathered church will reflect the need for a sense of stability. Over time those two distinct worship experiences will influence each other in powerful ways.

We must accept a heterodox church with a multitude of worship practices, which means that some people's worship will seem alien to us. We must accept that fact or we will never be inclusive. The unity of the church will have to be given up in terms of uniformity. That imperial idea of uniformity is no longer true. Our unity will be a common loaf and a common praxis. The bishop's job is to name the praxis at the local level.

Until our gathering includes the danger of persecution we will not understand the Cross. Churches need to be encouraged to live out the Gospel in their local setting, otherwise our worship has to do with something that is not connected to our real lives.

I want to see Prayer Book Studies 30 re-authorized. Ideally I would like to see a proliferation of materials produced over time rather than one limited set of materials replacing the last triennium's authorized texts each General Convention. For example, the forms for the "Prayers of the People" found in Prayer Book Studies 30 were used frequently by a seminary community in its worship. The present *Supplemental Liturgical Materials* are hard to use since the materials are all lumped together. The texts are not set out in ways that can be used easily. If we are going to get people to use supplemental materials they need to be "user friendly."

I have four specific thoughts about the future church and what the SLC is doing. First, the SLC should set out a clear set of criteria about what you feel is valid common prayer for the church. Second, you need to clarify what you mean by "inclusive liturgy" and an "inclusive church." There seems to be no common agreement about what that term really means. The fact that there are no people at this consultation representing those who are opposed to this process makes me question the use of the term. Third, I worry about the lack of clarity about the way we authorize liturgical texts in the church today. If everything is paperback and locally produced, why bother to have a Standing Liturgical Commission? Do we really need any authorization to do liturgy? Let different flowers bloom and blossom where they will and feed a lot of ideas into the "common market." Why then should there be one official body to feed those ideas out? Why not have different groups feed lots of things out to the church? Fourth, on the other hand, how far do we dare go in the decentralization of liturgy? How far do we see the vision of the church going in the abandonment of centralization of liturgy and other aspects of our life? Will everyone indeed do their own thing, or will there be some type of centralization? Our bishops are not like Roman Catholic bishops. Our bishops reflect their dioceses. "We get who we are." In the ecumenical movement old barriers are breaking down and new communities are forming. Ecumenism is cutting across all the boundaries. I'm puzzled about why you didn't invite local representatives of the larger ecumenical church. We can't do all this work on our own. To try to do so becomes another kind of exclusivity.

If you like Bosnia you will love what we are cooking up here— think about it.

My understanding is that we came here to throw out ideas. This was not designed to be a balanced conference to come up with an assessment of whether or not we should be involved in this work. Rather it was seen as one more step in an extensive process that has been going on now for some years. That process has involved and will continue to involve the encouragement of dialogue between persons with different perspectives. We have been listening to a wide variety of voices, and we need to continue to listen and respond in the future. This particular consultation, however, was designed to get at some theological fundamentals in conversation with persons who are deeply concerned about the issue of "inclusive" or "expansive" language and who have been praying the texts we have been producing.

What we are doing on the SLC today is working to provide liturgical materials for groups of people who want to use them. Through this process we see the enrichment of the church by providing a reservoir of prayers that express the tradition of the church using a full range of images and metaphors that are consonant with the tradition. In the church of the future "Eucharistic Prayers E and F" reflecting the desire for expansive language would be there alongside the present prayers in The Book of Common Prayer.

Note

1. *Supplemental Liturgical Materials*, pp. 43-47. See the rubrics for An Order for Celebrating the Holy Eucharist, BCP 1979, p. 400.